Devotions from A-Z

Written, Composed
and Photographed

by

Kenneth M. Lee

Old & New Testament Devotions for Everyday Living

Devotions from A-Z: by Kenneth Marshall Lee. Printed and bound in the United States of America. All composition rights reserved; however, devotional material may be used by non-profit theological institutions (churches, synagogues, etc . . .) for the purpose of teaching God's word and broadening spiritual knowledge. Material included herein shall not be used for commercial intent; neither shall it be reproduced for or within information storage and retrieval systems other than for one-time distribution among Bible study groups.

Printed by:
New Hanover Printing
2145 Wrightsville Ave.
Wilmington NC

Kenneth M. Lee
1382 Grandpa Lane.
Loris SC 29569
(843)756-1795

ISBN 0-9711850-1-5

About the Author: Kenneth Lee is a free lance author who lives in Loris SC and writes devotions for the local newspaper. He has been published in The Upper Room, Penned from the Heart, and various other publications. This is his second devotional book.

All Bible Scripture References are from the King James Version of the Holy Bible.

The Lord is nigh unto all those who call upon him, to all who call upon him in truth. He will fulfill the desire of those who fear him; he also will hear their cry, and will save them (Psalms 145: 18-19).

This Book is for you. May you ir
and Jesus Christ who are able
and salvation from bondage.

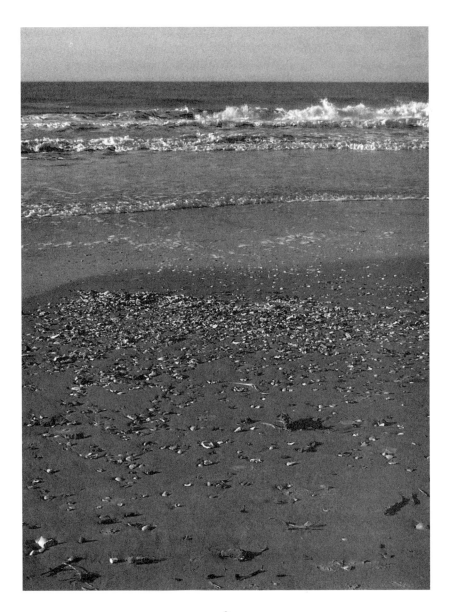

3

Introduction

Welcome to ***Devotions from A-Z.*** It is my sincere hope that you draw close to God as you read each devotion and apply it to your life.

The Bible is a guide for living, but its precepts, laws, and stories must be understood and practiced.

Devotions from A-Z is a good place to start studying the Holy Scriptures. The scriptures referenced and the devotions written are fundamental to the Judeo-Christian faith; however, the reader is encouraged to acquire an exhaustive concordance to the Bible, an expository, Hebrew and Greek Interlinear texts, and other translations of the Holy Scriptures. These resources are necessary to ascertain God's truth.

But all the studying in the world at this present time will not enable a person to find complete rest, peace, and happiness: the world is polluted with weaponry, mass communication devices, and toxins. Until these devices are eliminated and toxins cleaned of land, sea, and air, there will be little environmental peace.

Yet God has commanded us to be holy; neither shall ye defile the land.

As a young boy, raised by a mother with Cherokee Indian blood, being holy, righteous, and reverent towards God, man, and the environment went a long way towards finding peace and happiness. Learning about the herbs of the field and their natural remedies help keep me physically well. But having a full relationship with God the Father in Heaven is the ultimate answer for complete joy.

May God reveal Himself to you in *Devotions from A-Z.* May He grant you peace, wisdom, and happiness -- and understanding of just what He wants you to do in life. There is no greater joy -- than to serve the living God of the universe in truth and righteousness.

Table of Contents

5

Lying
Marriage
Mercy
Money
Obedience
Patience
Peace
Persecution
Prayer
Pride
Purpose
Rejected
Repentance
Righteousness
Safety
Salvation
Secrets
Sexual Relations
(Unmarried)
Sexual Relations
(Married)
Sickness
Sin
Sports
Strength
Stress
Suicide
Terror
Thankfulness
Travel
Trials
Truth
War
Wisdom
Work
Worry
Worship

Abandoned – Old Testament

And they took him, and cast him into a pit, and the pit was empty; there was no water in it.

Genesis 37: 24

Joseph was abandoned by his brothers and left in a pit do die until some merchantmen came along to lift him out.

Friends of family may abandon us, or even try to sell us, but being abandoned is a good time for drawing close to God.

Joseph prospered knowing God. He became a rich ruler in Egypt and in due time was reunited with his family.

The Bible says, For the Lord thy God is a merciful God, he will not forsake thee . . . (Deuteronomy 4: 31).

Reading scripture, praying, and listening to God's word helps us know God never abandons us.

Dear Lord, I thank You for being here with me when I call upon Your name. Forgive me if I have sinned and bring me back into fellowship with family, friends, and believers. Amen.

Abandoned – New Testament

Let your manner of life be without covetousness, and be content with such things as ye have; for he hath said, "I will never leave thee, nor forsake thee."

Hebrews 13: 5

God is with us but it helps to call on His name to know He is with us.

I felt abandoned after my wife left me in one afternoon but I awoke the next morning and went to the church building and in the middle of the hallway someone exclaimed, "God is here."

Well, God is here, and God's Son Jesus is here also.

"Abide in me, and I in you," Jesus says (John 15: 4).

So when feeling abandoned, consider Christ also as a friend who is here.

He said, "Ye are my friends, if ye do whatever I command you" (John 15: 14).

Christ at one time was abandoned by his disciples, yet he remained faithful to God (Mark 14: 50).

Dear Lord, I thank You for fellowship in Christ Jesus who has died for my sin and wants to be my friend. May I share this good news with other people who feel abandoned. Amen.

Other Bible References: Psalms 68: 5-6; 133: 1, 145: 18; Isaiah 41: 10; John 6: 37; 14: 23.

Adultery – Old Testament

And David sent messengers, and took her; and she came in unto him, and he lay with her; for she was purified from her uncleanness: and she returned unto her house.

2 Samuel 11: 4

David committed adultery with Bathsheba while his men were fighting a battle at Rabbah.

Perhaps if David would have been with his men, they might have won the battle—and David would have won the battle over the lust of his flesh.

But when David saw Bathsheba bathing on a rooftop and asked her into his home, lust conceived.

God wants all our attention on Him rather than a temptation to sin (Exodus 19; 3); otherwise, there will be discipline. David was confronted by Nathan the prophet about the sin and he went into deep mourning.

Consider reading Psalms 32 and 51 to see how David found God.

Dear Lord, Have mercy on me and forgive my sin. I humble myself from this sin of adultery. You are righteous. Restore this marriage by Your mercy, forgiveness, and truth. Amen.

Adultery – New Testament

And he saith unto them, "Whosoever shall put away his wife, and marry another, committeth adultery against her. And if a woman shall put away a husband, and marry another, she committeth adultery."

Mark 10: 11-12

Divorcing a spouse commits adultery because a faithful commitment of togetherness has been made in front of a holy God. God expects us to fulfill our vows.

But Jesus takes the issue of adultery further and says, "That whosoever looketh on a woman to lust after her hath committed adultery with her already in his heart" (Matthew 5: 28).

If adultery occurs, God has provided Jesus as a sacrifice for sin.

A woman, who was found in the act of adultery, was brought to Jesus for judgment, but Jesus did not condemn her (John 8: 1-14).

He instead received her and said, "Go, and sin no more."

Dear Father in Heaven, I come to You in humble confession and ask for forgiveness for my adulterous act. Restore this marriage I pray. Amen.

Other Bible References: Hosea 2; 1 Corinthians 7: 1-3; James 1: 14-15

Afraid – Old Testament

And Moses said unto the people, "Fear ye not, stand still, and see the salvation of the Lord, which he will show to you today."
Exodus 14: 13

God is the God of comfort and protection but when the Israelites looked up and saw Pharaoh's army chasing them, they became terrified. Their leader Moses told them to be still – and see the salvation of the Lord.

We need to be still and trust in God for comfort and salvation.

The people waited -- and God held back the waters of the Red Sea while they traveled safely to the other side. But Pharaoh's approaching army was overwhelmed by the water.

The Bible says, God is our refuge and strength, a very present help in time of trouble (Psalms 46: 1).

May we look to God to know He is in control and will protect and guide us to comfort.

Consider reading the Exodus story, Psalms 31, 46, and Isaiah 51: 1-16, to know God comforts His people.

Dear Lord, Your comfort is here and I trust You to help me. May I be still and know that you are a God of comfort. Amen.

Afraid – New Testament

The Lord is my helper, and I will not fear what men shall do unto me.

Hebrews 13: 6

Much of our fear comes from man who now has weaponry in the skies, terrorists on the streets, and deceivers in the marketplace, but the Bible advises us to fear God and not man.

For all flesh is like grass, and all the glory of man like the flower of grass. The grass withereth and its flower falleth away (1 Peter 1: 24).

It is God who has power to cast the soul into hell (Luke 12: 5); therefore, we need to make peace with God.

Comfort from God comes through Jesus Christ by the confession of sin. Acceptance of Christ brings the Holy Spirit as our Comforter (John 14: 26, 15: 26).

The last thing we fear is death, but Christ has defeated death by his resurrection from the grave (1 Corinthians 15: 54-57; Romans 8: 35-39).

Dear Lord, I praise You for Your Son Jesus who takes away sin. Christ is a Savior I can trust to give me peace. May I find comfort in Your holy place of refuge. Amen.

Other Bible References: Psalms 27: 1; 46: 10; 56: 3-4; 91: 15-16; 37: 4; 118; Proverbs 3: 25; Isaiah 55: 12; Romans 8: 15; 10: 13; John 14: 26; 16: 33; 2 Corinthians 1: 3-5: Hebrews 10: 26-36; 1 Peter 3: 14; 1 John 4: 18

Aging –Old Testament

And Moses was an hundred and twenty years old when he died; his eye was not dim, nor his natural force abated.
Deuteronomy 34: 7

Moses was a man who looked good at his death but he had actively worked for God in his life.

He walked up and down a mountain to receive God's commandments. He crossed a sea to lead His people to safety. And he camped in a wilderness to worship God.

We should be so active, but if we are sitting around and not doing anything, we are slowly aging.

A proverb says, By much slothfulness the building decayeth, and through idleness of the hands, the house droppeth through (Ecclesiastes 10: 18). Our house may be deteriorating along with our body if we don't get up to work for God.

Sharing God's word of life is what keeps us going, such as Moses who testified of God to the people before he died.

Dear Lord, I thank You for Your presence here today. My body sometimes gets weak, but Your spirit makes me strong. Amen.

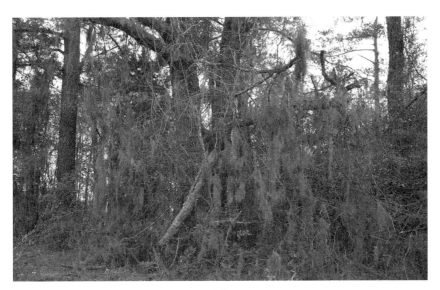

Aging – New Testament

And be renewed in the spirit of your mind; And that ye put on the new man, which after God is created in righteousness and true holiness.

Ephesians 4: 23-24

Upon acceptance as Christ as Savior, the old is indeed passed away and all things are new (2 Corinthians 5: 17).

A ruler named Nicodemus wanted to know how to put off the old person and become born again. He asked Jesus, "How can a man be born when he is old? Can he enter the second time into his mother's womb, and be born?"(John 3: 4).

Jesus said, (in the transliteration of the Greek language), "You must receive birth from above" (John 3: 7).

That's what we need: heavenly birth from above which allows us to actively witness for the living God.

Consider reading Ephesians 4: 22-32 for a renewal of your life.

Dear Father in Heaven, I thank You for the eternal life in Christ Jesus who is able to lift me up. Forgive my sins I pray through Christ and allow me to serve You in newness of spirit. Amen.

Other Bible References about Living a long life: Exodus 20: 12; Deuteronomy 30: 18; Job 11: 13-20; Psalms 103; Proverbs 3: 1-3; Luke 10: 25; John 3: 16; 7: 40; Romans 6-10; Colossians 3: 9-17;. 1 Peter 3: 10; Hebrews 6: 12; Prayer for old age: Psalms 71

Alcohol – Old Testament

" . . . neither have ye drunk wine or strong drink: that ye might know that I am the Lord your God."

Deuteronomy 29: 6

Abstaining from drinking fermented beverages brings us closer to know the Lord. Our bodies are not diluted with alcohol.

But it took a wilderness experience for the Israelites to realize God was their sole provider.

The Bible says, Wine is a mocker, strong drink is raging: and whosoever is deceived thereby is not wise (Proverbs 20: 1).

The wisest thing we can do is give our bodies nutritious food and pure drink. Then we can begin to serve the Lord in sincerity and truth.

Dear Lord, I trust You to keep me in the right place around the right people. May my body be purged of alcohol so I can be healthy for your service. Amen.

Alcohol – New Testament

"Verily I say unto you, I will drink no more of the fruit of the vine until that I drink it new in the kingdom of God."

Mark 14: 25

Jesus would not allow himself to drink vinegar for pleasure until he had performed the will of his Father in Heaven. In other words, work for God took priority in his life.

Knowing God's work has priority over our lives, we need to abstain from drinking excess alcohol.

The Bible says drunkards do not inherit the kingdom of God (1 Corinthians 6: 10). The New Testament further instructs us to be not drunk with wine, in which is excess, but be filled with the Spirit (Ephesians 5: 18).

The temptation to drink alcohol may be strong but God gives us the victory over temptation through Jesus Christ, who has defeated the lust of the flesh (Read Galatians 5: 17-24).

Dear Lord, May I abstain from alcohol and learn about God's word which gives me life. Grant me a new life in Christ Jesus. Amen.

Other Bible References: Isaiah 56-58; Psalms 104: 15; Proverbs 23: 29-30; John 6: 53-56; 7:37; Romans 6: 1-13; 1 Timothy 5: 23; 1 Peter 2: 11

Anger – Old Testament

And it came to pass, as soon as he came nigh unto the camp, that he saw the calf, and the dancing; and Moses anger waxed hot, and he cast the tables out of his hands, and brake them beneath the mount.

Exodus 32: 19

Moses got so angry at seeing the people worship a false idol that he threw down the tablets of stone containing God's Ten Commandments and they broke. That only made matters worse because he had to go back up the mountain and make two more tablets.

When we see things that make us angry, turning to God helps us find peace and guidance. The Bible says, Cease from anger, and forsake wrath, fret not thyself in any wise to do evil (Psalms 37: 8).

But God does get angry: He is angry with the wicked everyday (Psalms 7: 11). He had Moses divide the golden calf idolaters from those people who were on the Lord's side and three thousand idolaters were slain.

May we fear God enough to be on His side of anger.

Dear Lord, I pray you take this anger away so that I can have peace. I look to You for the right and wise thing to do. Amen.

17

Anger – New Testament

And they come to Jerusalem: and Jesus went into the temple, and began to cast out them that sold and bought in the temple, and overthrew the tables of the moneychangers, and the seats of them that sold doves.

Mark 11: 15

Jesus got angry at seeing God's holy temple being made a marketplace for the buying and selling of sacrificial offerings. We often get angry at seeing unrighteousness. Children may become disobedient, people may trespass against us, or leaders may become corrupt, but this is a good time for seeking God's wisdom; otherwise, we could become the victims of anger. The scribes and chief priests conspired to hurt Jesus and he had to leave town (Mark 11: 18).

If our anger is unjustified, Jesus says we are in danger of judgment and we should make peace with the adversary (Matthew 5: 22-26).

Possibly the best advice comes from the Book of Ephesians: Be ye angry, and sin not; let not the sun go down upon your wrath (Ephesians 4: 26).

Dear Lord, It makes me upset to see unrighteousness, but You are the great Judge and I know You will fix this situation. Grant me the wisdom to know what to do. Amen.

Other Bible References: Exodus 32: 22; Psalms 2: 11-12; Proverbs 15: 1; 19: 11; Matthew: 5: 12; Colossians 3: 8; Philippians 4: 7

Argument (Rebukement) – Old Testament

Thou shalt not hate thy brother in thine heart; thou shalt surely rebuke thy neighbor, and not allow sin upon him.

Leviticus 19: 17

Confronting someone about a sin may lead to an argument but we love our brothers and sisters enough to correct them if they are sinning.

The Bible says, Rebuke a wise man, and he will love thee (Proverbs 9: 8); Open rebuke is better than secret love (Proverbs 27: 5); Iron sharpeneth iron, so a man sharpeneth the countenance of his friend (Proverbs 27: 17).

However, we should be wise to search out God's scriptures before correcting someone: it may be that we are the ones who need corrected.

In contrast to those proverbs, there are people that should not be rebuked. Answer not a fool according to his folly, lest thou also be like unto him (Proverbs 26: 4); Rebuke not a scorner, lest he hate thee (Proverbs 9: 8).

Dear Lord, May I refrain from debates and disputes, yet if I must argue, may I do so in the spirit of brotherhood and righteousness. Amen.

19

Argument-New Testament

I told you, and you believed not; the works that I do in my Father's name, they bear witness of me.

John 10: 25

Jesus found himself in the middle of arguments on several occasions: he argued for new Sabbath day regulations and his identify being the Son of God.

If we are committed to God, we will be arguing for righteous principles.

The Bible advises us to rebuke liars and hypocrites sharply, that they may be sound in the faith (read Titus 1: 9--2: 15).

Arguments take place daily in courtrooms, business offices, homes, and on playgrounds. These are good opportunities to proclaim righteousness but also witness for God.

But the Apostle Paul says to do all things without murmurings and disputings, that ye may be blameless and harmless, the sons of God without rebuke . . . (Philippians 2: 14-15).

Dear Lord, It upsets me to argue, but at times this has to be done. May I receive the strength and facts to argue righteously with You as witness. Amen.

Other Bible References: Psalms 39: 11; Mark 8: 31-33; 1 Timothy 5: 1

Believe – Old Testament

And he believed in the Lord; and he counted it to him for righteousness.

Genesis 15: 6

Abraham believed in the Lord because he received a vision that came true: he inherited land and a family.

We might also receive a vision from God that comes true, if we know God.

But obtaining God's vision is not without trials and troubles. For Abraham, a famine occurred and he had to travel to Egypt to find food. Further, Abraham's wife, Sarah, mocked the suggestion they would have a child after a visit by God's angel.

Satan will do anything to stop us from obtaining God's blessings, but when God ordains something, it will come true by belief.

The Bible says, "The Lord of hosts hath sworn, saying, Surely as I have thought, so shall it come to pass, and as I have purposed, so shall it stand," (Isaiah. 14: 24).

Dear Lord, I believe You are here when I call on Your name, and You will perform that which You have shown me. May I be a faithful servant who carries out Your mission for my life. Amen.

Believe – New Testament

Jesus said unto her, "I am the resurrection, and the life; he that believeth in me, though he were dead, yet shall he live."

John 11: 25

Believing in Christ frees us from the fear of death and the bondage from sin.

For he hath made him, who knew no sin, to be sin for us, that we might be made the righteousness of God in him (2 Corinthians 5: 21).

It's up to us to believe, but normally some tragedy takes place before we call on Jesus.

A nobleman's son was at the point of death, but Jesus his father that the son would live, and when the nobleman returned home, servants met him on the way and confirmed the boy was alive (John 4: 46-54).

Many people saw the miracles Jesus performed and they believed (John 2: 23). Jesus raised the lame, opened the eyes of the blind, loosened the tongues of the mute, and forgave sin.

God's powers are with us -- when we believe.

John the Baptist told the Levites and priests, "Behold, the lamb of God, who taketh away the sin of world" (John 1: 29).

Dear God, I believe in the resurrection of Christ to take away my sins and give me salvation. Amen.

Other Bible References: Exodus 4: 4-5; Mark 9: 23; John 3: 16; 6: 47; 10: 37-38; chapter 14; Acts 16: 31; Romans 10: 9; Ephesians 1: 3-23; Hebrews 11: 6

Building – Old Testament

Make thee an ark of gopher wood; rooms shalt thou make in the ark, and shalt pitch it within and without with pitch.

Genesis 6: 14

God instructed Noah to build an ark because a catastrophic flood was coming to remove all the evil from the earth.

The ark would have a big door, a window, and it would be three stories high -- to hold all of Noah's family and pairs of all known animals.

But when God builds things, He builds them just right,

The Bible says, "Except the Lord build the house, they labor in vain that build it; except the Lord keep the city, the watchman waketh but in vain," (Psalms 127: 1).

May we look to the Lord for building shelter and transportation but also our spiritual lives around His Word of truth. God designed His Word to give us a foundation for a good life.

He will keep us safe as he did Noah, who found grace in the eyes of the Lord and was saved from the flood.

Dear Father in Heaven, May I build according to Your plan and make a sure foundation. Thank You for Your Word of life. Amen.

Building – New Testament

"In my Father's house are many mansions . . . ."

John 14: 2

A good place to start building a life with Jesus is by reading the 14th Chapter of the Book of John and knowing there is a place in heaven reserved for those who believe.

But Jesus says, " . . . no man cometh to the Father but by me (John 14: 6).

Lust and sin are defeated (Ephesians 4: 21-24); and a new life of righteousness begins upon the acceptance of Christ (2 Corinthians 5: 17).

Our lives become complete when the love of Jesus indwells us and the Holy Spirit blesses those around us.

Our feet walk with grace, our words are seasoned with truth, and our actions show mercy

Dear God, I praise You for being here and building my faith in Jesus. May I complete the work You show me and may I build using the right materials of faith and trust. Amen.

Other Biblical References: Matthew 7: 24; 17: 18; 1 Corinthians 3: 9-17

Children – Old Testament

And ye shall teach them your children, speaking of them when thou sittest in thine house, and when thou walkest by the way, when thou liest down, and when thou riseth up.

Deuteronomy 11: 19

God wants us to tell our children about His statutes but also about how He delivered His people from slavery:

With a mighty hand, and an outstretched arm, He brought them out of bondage (Deuteronomy 28: 6).

Teaching children to fear and respect God will multiply their days upon earth (Deut. 11: 21). However, children will need discipline.

The Bible says, Withhold not correction from a child . . . (Proverbs 23: 13). The rod and reproof give wisdom, but a child left to himself bringeth his mother to shame (Proverbs 29: 15).

God gives us instruction on how to raise children. It's up to us to apply it and be reverent.

Dear Lord, Thank You for being here and helping me raise my children. Bless us as a family Lord, have mercy on us, and keep us together. Amen.

Children –New Testament

And ye fathers, provoke not your children to wrath: but bring them up in the nurture and admonition of the Lord.

Ephesians 6: 4

God wants us to encourage our children and not be angry at them. That means to speak positively and show them the right way to do things.

The Bible says, And the servant of the Lord must not strive, but be gentle unto all men, apt to teach, patient (2 Timothy 2: 24).

Children need to see our patience. They need to see our wisdom, and they need to see God in all that we do, because they will imitate our actions.

Consider reading Bible stories children and attending church where children can interact with each other.

Jesus, as a young child, was in the temple daily learning about God and gaining wisdom.

Dear Lord, Keep us together in the love and mercy of Jesus, who died for our sins. I will encourage my child daily with Your help. Amen.

Other Bible References: Psalms 119: 9; Proverbs 10: 1; 13: 24; 20: 7; 22: 6, 15

Confession – Old Testament

When I kept silence, my bones waxed old through my roaring all the day long.

Psalms 32: 3

King David is talking about his pain of keeping silent about his sin.

Our bones will become old and pains will exist if we don't confess sin.

The Bible says, He that covereth his sins shall not prosper, but whoso confesseth and forsaketh them shall have mercy (Proverbs 28: 13).

God wants us to confess sins so we can have mercy and life, and God is faithful to forgive our sins when we bow to Him in confession (2 Chronicles 7: 14).

Dear God, "Have mercy upon me, O God, according to Thy loving kindness: according unto the multitude of Thy tender mercies blot out my transgressions. Wash me thoroughly from mine iniquity, cleanse me from my sin. For I acknowledge my transgressions and my sin is ever before me;" (Psalms 51: 1-3). Amen.

Confession – New Testament

If we confess our sins, he is faithful and just to forgive us our sins, and to cleanse us from all unrighteousness.

1 John 1: 9

When confession of sin takes place, there is an acknowledgment of sin. An action has been compared with the law of God and a transgression has occurred.

Only a holy God can completely redeem sin. This is why God sent His Son Jesus to earth in the form of sinless man from the virgin Mother Mary to be a perfect sacrifice for sin.

Consider talking to God in private prayer when sin begins to overflow. Jesus said to go to the Father in secret and He will reward you openly (Matthew 6: 6).

The Bible also says, That if thou shalt confess with they mouth the Lord Jesus, and shalt believe in thine heart that God that raised him from the dead, thou shalt be saved (Romans 10: 9).

Dear God, I bow down before You in humble confession. Please forgive me. I acknowledge my transgression and commit myself to Your righteous ways. Thank You for Jesus who died for me. Amen.

Other Bible References: 2 Chronicles 7: 14; Matthew 10: 32; Romans 14: 11-12

Confidence – Old Testament

"Have not I commanded thee? Be strong and of good courage; be not afraid, neither be thou dismayed; for the Lord thy God is with thee wherever thou goest."

Joshua 1: 9

Joshua assumed command of the Israelites and received confidence from the Lord to lead the people across the Jordan river to the promised land of Palestine. But Joshua knew God from when he was a young man: he had worshipped in the tabernacle and saw Him in a cloudy pillar (Ex. 33: 11).

We should get so intimate with God. We should know that God is our confidence. The Bible says, For the Lord shall be thy confidence, and keep thy foot from being taken (Proverbs 3: 26).

But if sin is in our lives, we need to have it removed before we can get God's confidence. The Israelites had been defeated in their battle at Kadesh-Barnea because of their sin. Moses told the people, "Go not up, for the Lord is not among you; that ye be not smitten before your enemies" (Numbers 14: 42).

Following Joshua, who had God's confidence, the Israelites crossed the Jordan river and entered their land of promise.

Dear Lord, You are my confidence, and not man. I put You first in my life to achieve great things for Your glory. Amen.

29

Jesus answered and said unto him, "If a man love me, he will keep my words; and my Father will love him, and we will come in unto him, and make our abode with him."

John 14: 23

Having Jesus and God in our lives gives us great confidence. God is an advocate for our sins, and Jesus is the propitiation for them (1 John 2: 1-2).

When we abide in Jesus and perform his sayings, then whatever we ask, it shall be done (John 15: 7). Jesus intercedes for us (Hebrews 7: 25), and the Holy Spirit will also intercede for us according to the will of God (Romans 8: 26). This is great confidence.

Prayer bolsters our confidence. God shows us what to do, where to go, how to get there, and how to get things done— before it all takes place. And we know what God purposes will come true.

Beloved, if our heart condemn us not, then we have confidence toward God (1 John 3: 21).

Dear Lord, Thank You for giving me confidence through Christ Jesus. I can do all things through Christ who strengthens me. Amen.

Other Bible References: Psalms 118: 6; Proverbs 14: 16, 26; Micah 7: 5; Mark 9: 23; John 15: 1-6; Philippians 4: 13; Psalm for Confidence: Psalms 3; Triumphant Faith: Psalm 27

Confusion – Old Testament

The proud have had me greatly in derision, yet have I not declined from thy law.

Psalms 119: 51

Satan's desire is to keep a person constantly confused but knowing God's law rejects moral confusion: His statutes are right.

The Bible says, Thou shalt keep, therefore, his statutes, and his commandments, which I command thee this day, that it may go well with thee (Deuteronomy 4: 40).

But many of us are stubborn, which may cause us to flee seven ways before enemies, be consumed with madness, and have sorrow of mind (read Deuteronomy 28: 15-68).

Consider humbling yourself to God when confused and remember that God is always in control.

The simplicity of life's requirement might be summed up in Micah 6: 8: "What does the Lord require of thee but do to justice, love mercy, and walk humbly with thy God?" (Micah 6: 8).

Dear Father in Heaven, I thank You for your truth, for having a stable mind, and knowing right from wrong. May I humble myself under Your great hand so that I am at peace. Amen.

Wherefore, it is also contained in the scriptures, Behold, I lay in Zion a chief corner stone, elect, precious: and he that believeth on him shall not be confounded.

1 Peter 4: 6

Believing in Jesus eliminates religious confusion because he is a total sacrifice for man's sins (Hebrews 10: 1-14). He eliminates worldly confusion because he said the devil was a liar from the beginning (John 8: 12-59). And he eliminates personal confusion because he saves us from sin and gives us security upon death.

We are instructed to be sober-minded (1 Thessalonians 5: 4-11). Scripture also says, That we henceforth be no more children, tossed to and fro, and carried about with every wind of doctrine . . . But, speaking the truth in love . . . (Ephesians 4: 14-15).

When burdened with confusion, we need to search out the truth, for the truth makes us free (John 8: 32).

Man has made many devices and tried to distort truth but we are encouraged to remain strong and employ a shield of faith against the works of the devil (Ephesians 6: 10-20).

Dear Father in Heaven,, I put my trust in You to reject confusion and rest in the truth. Amen.

Other Bible References: Psalms 71: 24; Proverbs 8: 20; 24: 10; Mark 12: 29-31; 13: 22; John 3: 11; 1 Corinthians 1: 26-30; 14: 33 ;Romans 14: 22-23; Philippians 4: 1; Titus 2; Revelation 12: 9; The Simplicity of Christ: 2 Corinthians 11: 3

Courage – Old Testament

And David said to Saul, 'Let no man's heart fail because of him; thy servant will go and fight with this Philistine."

1 Samuel 17: 32

David had little fear of fighting the giant Goliath because he knew God was with him. He had already killed a lion and a bear with God.

So David invoked the name of God when facing Goliath: he slung a stone at Goliath's forehead and Goliath went down.

When there are giants in our lives, we should also invoke His name for courage.

The Bible says, Through God we shall do valiantly; for he it is who shall tread down our enemies (Psalms 60: 12).

God is a partner we can count trust to defeat the enemy.

Dear Lord, With You, all things are indeed possible. Strengthen me to be courageous for Your sake. Amen.

Courage – New Testament

But Peter and John answered and said unto them, "Whether it is right in the sight of God to hearken unto you more than unto God, judge ye."

Acts 4: 19

The Apostles showed great courage talking back to the Sanhedrin council despite being threatened with jail and beatings for preaching Jesus was a Savior.

Testifying about Christ has it dangers and Jesus confirms this when he says, "Whosoever will come after me, let him deny himself, and take up his cross, and follow me (Mark 8: 34).

Each of us who believes in Christ sacrifices a life of personal desire to fulfill God's desire.

The Apostles turned to God in prayer. "And now, Lord, behold their threatenings; and grant unto thy servants, that with all boldness they may speak thy word" (Acts 4: 29).

When faced with fear, consider calling on God in prayer and Jesus for courage and strength.

The Apostle Paul said, "I can do all things through Christ who strengtheneth me" (Philippians 4: 13).

Dear Lord, Your presence here encourages me and I thank You in advance of defeating the enemy by righteousness and truth. Have mercy on us I pray. Amen.

Other Bible References: Psalms 27: 14; 31: 24; John 16: 33; 1 Corinthians 16: 13; Ephesians 6: 10

Crying – Old Testament

And she sat apart from him, and lifted up her voice, and wept.
Genesis 21: 16

Hagar is crying because her child is dying of thirst and she has gone off a short distance to not see his death. But God comes into Hagar's life and tells her He has heard the voice of the lad and shows her a well for water.

God knew the sad condition of the child and Hagar, and He knows our situation.

The Bible says, God is nigh unto those who are of a broken heart, and saveth such as be of a contrite spirit (Psalms 34: 18).

Sad situations are good times for being close to God. He comforts us with His presence and encourages us to get stronger by His guidance.

Dear Father in Heaven, I thank You for being close to me in my tears. Comfort me and restore my strength I pray. Amen.

Crying – New Testament

Jesus wept.

John 11: 35

Jesus cried because his friend Lazarus had died but he didn't weep for long because he wanted to see where Lazarus was taken to invoke God's glory.

Death of a loved one or a sad circumstance may make us weep but it's also a good time to witness for God's presence. Jesus went to the cave and ordered Lazarus to come forth for the glory of God.

When tears flow and life seems sad, look for Jesus in the midst. The Bible says the lamb Jesus is in the midst of the throne . . . and shall lead them to fountains of living waters: and God shall wipe away all tears from their eyes (Revelation 7: 17).

The Bible also says, Blessed are they that mourn, for they shall be comforted (Matthew 5: 4).

Dear Father in Heaven, I thank You for being here amidst my tears. and I praise You for Jesus who gives me the strength to live for Your sake. Amen.

Other Bible References: Job 16: 16-17; Psalms 6: 8-9; 30: 3; 126: 5; Joel 2: 12; James 4: 8-10; Revelation 7: 1; 21: 4

Death – Old Testament

And it came to pass after these things, Joshua, the son of Nun, the servant of the Lord, died, being one hundred and ten years old.

Joshua 24: 29

Joshua testified of God's saving presence in front of the leaders of Israel and recollected events of the past that had led to the people's freedom before he died (Joshua 24: 1-13).

We might also give testimony about God's presence but if we have differences with God, now is a good time for acknowledging them and asking forgiveness. The Bible says, "For in death there is no remembrance of thee; in the grave who shall give thee thanks?" (Psalms 6: 5).

Being forgiven by God allows us to freely testify of His presence. Friends and family might be saved by our testimony and it will give them a good direction for the future.

Dear Heavenly Father, I thank You for life, and I give testimony about Your presence that kept me. Have mercy upon me Lord, and grant me peace and rest. Amen.

Death – New Testament

For God so loved the world, that he gave his only begotten Son, that whosoever believeth in Him should not perish, but have everlasting life.

John 3: 16

Jesus overcomes death by his resurrection from the grave but many people many had trouble believing. '

The Apostle Thomas wanted to see the nail prints and the blood in Christ's body. When he saw, he believed (John 20: 25-29).

God forbid us to see wounds and blood before we believe in the risen Christ.

When the shadows become longer, the body moves slower, and the vision blurs, Jesus is still here to give us life after death.

Jesus says, "I am the resurrection and the life: he that believeth in me, though he were dead, yet shall he live. And whosoever liveth and believeth in me shall never die. Believest thou this?" (John 11: 25-26).

The choice is ours. Resting in death in the arms of a loving Savior for an eternity is worth bowing before Him in life.

Dear Lord, I praise You for sending Jesus to free me from the pains of death and give me peace. I believe in the Holy Ghost, the forgiveness of sins, and life everlasting. Amen.

Other Bible References: Genesis 3: 19; Psalms 88: 10-12; John 11: 25; Romans 6: 11;: Ephesians 2: 5; 5: 14

Debt – Old Testament

> *. . . Thy servant my husband is dead; and thou knowest that thy servant did fear the Lord: and the creditor is come to take my two sons to be bondmen.*
>
> *1 Kings 4: 1*

A woman was in debt, so she looked to the man of God Elisha for some wisdom. Elisha told her to go home and divide what little oil she had and put it in separate containers to sell.

Wisdom suggests we divide what little we have and make it last longer or sell something to pay off a debt.

But the only debt we should have is praising God each and every day and witnessing for Him. Psalms 23 tells us to trust the Lord for our needs: "The Lord is my shepherd, I shall not want [lack]" (Psalms 23: 1).

If we have borrowed a tangible asset, we don't want to be known as a wicked people (Psalms 37: 21); so we should pay on what we owe.

The writer of Ecclesiastes gives us good advice: Better is it that thou shouldest not vow, then that thou shouldest vow and not pay (Ecclesiastes 5: 5).

Dear Father in Heaven, Please show me the way to repay this debt. May I never borrow again. I trust You to supply my needs. Amen.'

Debt – New Testament

"The servant, therefore, fell down, and worshiped him, saying, 'Lord, have patience with me, and I will pay thee all'."

Matthew 18: 26

Jesus tells a parable about a poor servant owing money to his master and the master requiring payment. The poor servant bowed down before his master and was granted mercy. But the same poor servant had a man who owed him money – and he would not forgive. The servant's lord got angry with him and sent interrogators, saying the servant had been forgiven yet would not forgive. So the servant was sent to his creditors' tormentors – and would work to pay off the debt.

A portion of Christ's prayer says, "And forgive us our debts, as we forgive our debtors" (Matthew 6: 12). If we ask for mercy, we should give mercy to others.

But if we are in debt to sin, Christ's death on the cross paid the price. Upon confession and redemption of sin, we are free to serve and worship the living God (Romans 3: 24-26; 1 Peter 1: 18-19).

Dear Lord, I ask for patience paying off this debt and I promise never to get in monetary debt again. I am reminded to witness for You about the freedom Jesus gives by his sacrifice for sin. Amen.

Other Bible References: Psalms 37: 21; Proverbs 22: 7, Romans 3: 23-24; 13: 8

Devil – Old Testament

Now there was a day when the Sons of God came to present themselves before the Lord, and Satan came also among them.

Job 1: 6

Satan is ever present in the world and likes to make a big show but it was God who instigated this plan over his servant Job to show power.

God has power over Satan but we must obey Him and stay separate from sin. (Job was not so innocent in this drama because he was offering sacrifices for the sins of his children.)

The Psalmist says, Because thou hast made the Lord, who is my refuge, even the Most High, thy habitation, There shall no evil befall thee, neither shall any plague come nigh thy dwelling (Psalms 91: 9-10).

When Satan comes around, stay around God's throne for victory but it may mean to repent in ashes and dust like Job.

Dear Father in Heaven, Thank You for having power over the devil. When Satan comes around, I look to You for help. Protect me and have mercy on me Lord. Amen.

41

Devil – New Testament

Be sober, be vigilant; because your adversary the devil, as a roaring lion, walketh about, seeking whom he may devour: whom resist steadfast in the faith, knowing that the same afflictions are accomplished in our brethren that are in the world.

1 Peter 5: 8-9

In order to resist the devil, we must understand his traits: he lies, cheats, steals, murders, and deceives. He is presumptuous, prideful, malignant, wise, envious, and covetous.

The good news is that Christ has defeated the devil. When tempted to sin by the devil in the wilderness, Jesus quoted God's word and told the devil that God could not be tempted -- but to go away and worship God.

Christ further conquered the devil when he took the people's sins to the cross and put them to death.

The devil was in a young man who was being thrown into fire and water, but Jesus rebuked the evil spirit and it came out (Matthew 17: 18).

. The power of Jesus in holiness, righteousness, and resurrection from the dead defeats devils.

Dear Lord, I confront the devil in the power of Jesus Christ and Your righteousness. but I am also humble enough to let You drive him away. Amen.

Other Bible References, Genesis 3: 14; Isaiah 14: 15; Zechariah 3: 1; Matthew 17: 15; Mark 12: 17; Romans 16: 20; 1 Timothy 3: 7; Ephesians 4: 27; James 4: 7

Disability – Old Testament

And as he passed over Penuel the sun rose upon him, and he halted upon his thigh.

Genesis 32: 31

Jacob became disabled when he failed to bless God and an angel knocked his thigh out of joint.

We may become disabled from failing to bless God; or possibly we are disabled from birth or have suffered a tragic accident, but we are whole in the spirit to glorify God.

Glorifying God can be done in many ways: nursing, ministering, constructing, writing, or speaking.

The Bible says God had formed Jacob for His purpose -- to give Him glory (Isaiah 43: 1-13). And God has formed us for His purpose and glory.

Jacob was made whole in his faith, and he visited brother Esau with blessings.

Dear Lord, I am complete in You, fully able to pray and serve You. Have mercy upon me and may You be glorified in all that I do. Amen.

Disability – New Testament

. . . There was given to me a thorn in the flesh, the messenger of Satan to buffet me, lest I should be exalted above measure.
2 Corinthians 12: 7

The Apostle Paul felt his disability kept him humble. Being disabled keeps us humble because we move slower and feel pain, yet God has given us the spirit of grace through Jesus to bear it (2 Corinthians 12: 9); and Jesus intercedes for our suffering (Hebrews 4: 14-16).

But if we don't know Jesus, we need to learn about him to complete our faith.

An impotent man lay by the waters to get completely healed but no one would help, but Jesus came along and said, "Arise, take up thy bed, and walk" (John 5: 1-9). The man was healed.

The sick, disabled, and impotent came to Jesus and were healed (Matthew 15: 30).

Disabled in the world but God is able to do exceedingly above all we think or ask when we yield our members to Him (Ephesians 3:14-21).

Dear Heavenly Father, Everyday is difficult in this body, but everyday is precious because You fill me with the spirit to serve You. May I use my body to produce good works and testify of Your Holy name. Amen.

Other Bible Reference Scriptures: Psalms 25; 88; 100: 3; Isaiah 43: 7, 53: 5; Psalms 100: 3; 138: 8; Matthew 18: 8; Luke 5: 24-25; John 9: 3; 17: 23; Romans 8: 26; 2 Corinthians 12: 12-26; Colossians 2: 9-10; Hebrews 4: 15; 7: 25

Discouragement – Old Testament

. . . And he requested for himself that he might die, and said, "It is enough!"

1 Kings 19: 4

Elijah was discouraged because King Ahab's wife Jezebel was seeking to kill him, so he walked out a day's distance in the desert and sat under a juniper tree hoping to die.

But God sent an angel to touch Elijah and told him to get up, eat, and continue on the journey.

We may feel so discouraged we want to die but God is here.

In the heat of the day, under the shade of the Almighty, we might hear the words that give us new life: "Arise, eat, and continue on the journey."

Dear Lord, I am encouraged by Your presence here. Let me be faithful to achieve that which You want me to do in my life. Amen.

Discouragement – New Testament

And saith unto them, "My soul is exceeding sorrowful unto death: tarry ye here, and watch."

Mark 14: 34

Jesus was discouraged because the time was drawing near for him to die for the people's sins, and then he found his disciples sleeping at a time when soldiers would soon come to arrest him.

But he looked to God for encouragement. He walked off a short distance and bowed in prayer.

We become discouraged in a world of poverty, sickness, war, and tragedy, but God is still here for encouragement in prayer.

He gave Jesus the strength to follow complete His calling and He gives us strength to achieve great things for His name's sake.

We are also encouraged to exhort one another, as we see the day approaching (Hebrews 10: 25).

Dear Lord, I am discouraged about the events taking place around me; but I know You are in charge. You are my strength to perform good works and glorify Your name. Amen.

Other Bible References: Deuteronomy 1: 21; Numbers 32: 7; John 10: 10; Colossians 3: 21; James 5: 13-16

Divorce – Old Testament

. . . then let him write her a bill of divorcement, and give it in her hand, and send her out of his house.
Deuteronomy 24: 1

Divorce was permitted in the Old Testament when the man felt his wife was unfavorable towards him.

But the man had been given power over the woman (Genesis 3: 16); he had the authority to void or accept her words (Numbers 30: 6-8).

From the beginning, divorce was not meant to be; the man and woman were created in God's image to multiply on the face of the earth (Genesis 1: 17).

Before getting divorced, make sure a relationship with God is intact: we do not want to be divorced from God.

The Lord our God is one Lord (Deuteronomy 6: 4).

Dear Lord, You are the one I should truly be married to but I also pray for my spouse to come to know Your love, mercy, and fellowship. Amen.

Divorce – New Testament

But if the unbelieving depart, let him depart. A brother or a sister is not under bondage in such cases; but God hath called unto peace.

1 Corinthians 7: 15

The Apostle Paul tries to justify the separation of an unbelieving spouse by saying there will be peace without bondage -- but marriage is a bond -- and Christ Jesus says a spouse should not divorce but in the case of fornication (Matthew 5: 32).

Jesus further says, "What therefore God hath joined together, let man not put asunder;" (Matthew 19: 6).

Nevertheless, problems do occur within a marriage; yet scripture encourages us to be kind one to another, tenderhearted, forgiving one another, even as God, for Christ's sake, hath forgiven you (Ephesians 4: 32).

Pray for a separated mate to find Jesus. Regardless of what happens in a domestic marriage, Jesus is a mate for life.

Wherefore, my brethren, ye also are become dead to the law by the body of Christ; that ye should be married to another, even to him who is raised from the dead, that we should bring forth fruit unto God (roOmans 7: 4).

Dear Lord, If I have sinned, forgive me of sin and let me reconcile with You. I love you Lord, and I hope my mate loves You and finds Your mercy. Amen.

Other Bible References: Romans 7: 4

Drugs – Old Testament

"Is not this the fast that I have chosen – to loose the bands of wickedness, to undo the heavy burdens, and to let the oppressed go free, and that ye break every yoke?"

Isaiah 58: 6

Breaking the drug habit requires that something be put in its place, like faith in the living God. He is fully able to give spiritual joy in life and keep the body nutritionally healthy.

Read Isaiah 56-58 to learn about how separation to God brings blessings.

In another reading, a psalmist said he called on the name of the Lord and was saved from death; he was brought low -- but the Lord helped him ((Psalm 116: 4-8).

When the body becomes free of drugs and the mind fully dependent on God, then joy will indeed break forth as the morning sun and good health will flourish as a tree besides living waters (Isaiah 58: 8).

Dear Father in Heaven, You are the way for life and I commit my ways to You. I confess my inadequacies and solely trust You to provide me peace, happiness, and the work I need for a prosperous life. Amen.

Drugs – New Testament

And they that are Christ's have crucified the flesh with the affections and lust.

Galatians 5: 24

Christ Jesus gives us power over the temptation to take drugs because he has crucified the lusts of the flesh, risen from the dead, and intercedes for us.

When a temptation comes to take a drug, look to Christ, who sits on the right hand side of God (Hebrews 1: 3). The devil has been defeated but it takes our faith in the living Christ to rebuke and send him away.

Our bodies are to be used for God's purpose and service (1 Corinthians 6: 20; Romans 12).

Consider also reading the 1st and 2nd chapter of Ephesians to see Christ's power over fleshly lusts.

God is faithful, who will not suffer you to be tempted above that ye are able, but will, with the temptation, also make a way to escape, that ye may be able to bear it (1 Corinthians 10: 13).

Dear Lord, I confess my sin and call on Your name for help. Have mercy on me and renew me in the right spirit to love Jesus in body, mind, and soul. I can do all this though Christ who strengthens me. Amen.

Other Bible References: 2 Chronicles 7: 14; 1 Corinthians 9: 27: 2 Peter 1: 7; Nutrition: Romans 14.

Eating – Old Testament

And he humbled thee, and suffered thee to hunger, and fed thee with manna, which thou knewest not, that he might make thee know that man doth not live by bread only, but by every word that proceedeth out of the mouth of the Lord doth man live.

Deuteronomy 8: 3

God caused the Hebrews to hunger temporarily so they would learn that man does not live by bread alone -- but by the word of God.

In times of famine, we might take biblical advice from the psalmist, Trust in the Lord, and do good; so shalt thou dwell in the land, and verily thou shalt be fed (Psalms 37: 3).

Consider also the words of Agur in the Book of Proverbs: "Remove far from me vanity and lies; give me neither poverty nor riches; feed me with food convenient for me (Proverbs 30: 8).

A gift from God is to be able to work and eat, but we are expected to acknowledge His presence.

Dear Father in Heaven, I thank You for bread from earth, but I also thank You for bread from heaven. Your Word feeds me the wisdom I need to work and testify of Your saving presence. Amen.

Eating – New Testament

Hast thou faith? have it to thyself before God. Happy is he that condemneth not himself in that thing which he alloweth.
Romans 14: 22

The 14th Chapter of Romans basically states that eating something that strengthens the faith in God is good, but eating something that causes a person to stumble or make mistakes is not good; therefore, God should be consulted before eating.

The Bible also says the kingdom of God is not meat and drink but righteousness, peace, and joy in the Holy Ghost (Romans 14: 17).

Jesus said not to worry about food for the body: the birds of the air neither sow, reap, nor gather into barns, but the Lord feeds them (Matthew 6: 28).

In other words, we are to focus on what God wants us to do in the spirit of life and He will feed us our daily bread.

Dear Heavenly Father, I praise you for showing me what food is acceptable for my body, but also for Jesus who fills me with heavenly bread that gives me life everlasting. Amen.

Other Bible References: Leviticus 11; John 6: 51; Hebrews 13: 9

Enemies – Old Testament

And Saul cast the javelin; for he said, I will smite David even to the wall with it. And David avoided out of his presence twice.
1 Samuel 18: 11

King Saul considered David an enemy after David slayed the giant Goliath in battle and gained fame among the people.

We may have enemies like Saul when someone becomes jealous or resentful, but that's a good time for turning to God.

David prayed for the Lord to have vengeance on Saul, "As the Lord liveth, the Lord shall smite him, or his day shall come to die; or he shall descend into battle, and perish" (1 Samuel 26: 10).

God will have vengeance on His adversaries (Deuteronomy 32: 35); He is an enemy to enemies (Numbers 23: 22-33). But this protection only comes from being obedient to God and following His statutes.

Saul died in another battle and David was spared the guilt of retaliation because he prayed to God.

Dear Heavenly Father, Please spare me from this enemy's anger and take him away from me. Confront this enemy in righteousness and judgment as I keep You first in my life. Amen.

Enemies – New Testament

And the Pharisees went forth and straightway took counsel with the Herodians against him, how they might destroy him.

Mark 3: 6

Jesus became an enemy of the Pharisees when he started healing on the Sabbath Day of rest. Scribes and priests also considered Jesus an enemy because he was teaching a new doctrine (Luke 19: 47). And the Jews sought to slay Jesus for claiming to be the Son of God (John 5: 18).

We will have enemies for following Jesus. He was a righteous man who proclaimed truth from God, and many people became offended. They still do.

But Jesus says to bless your enemies and pray for them who despitefully use you (Matthew 5: 43-44). Jesus knew that God entreats us favorably when we pray good things for other people.

Giving an enemy over to God in prayer allows us to go and complete the work God has for us in life.

Dear Heavenly Father, I thank You for Your intercession here to help me be at peace. May my enemy come to know Your peace also through the precious blood of Jesus, who died for us. Amen.

Other Bible References: Exodus 23: 4; Job 31: 29; Psalms 68: 1; 92: 9; Proverbs 25: 21; 1 Corinthians 15: 25-26; Revelation 21: 8

Evil - Old Testament

But it shall to come to pass, if thou wilt not hearken unto the voice of the Lord thy God, to observe to do all his commandments and his statutes which I command thee this day, that all these curses shall come upon thee, and overtake thee.

Deuteronomy 28: 15

God knows about evil because He created it and He threatens man with it upon disobedience to the commandments (Genesis 2: 9; Isaiah 45: 7).

The traits of evils are something no man would want part of as they include cursing, destruction, pestilence, fever, burning, madness, and slavery (Deuteronomy 28: 15-68).

But fortunately for us, God has power over all these evils. We need to only get right with God to be spared of them.

The fear of the Lord is to hate evil (Proverbs 8: 13), and we are advised to depart from evil and do good (Psalm 37: 27; Proverbs 3: 7).

Innumerable evils encompassed a psalmist -- iniquities had consumed and shamed him -- but he made the Lord his trust for mercy and salvation (read Psalm 40).

Dear Lord, Thank You for having control over evil. May Your righteousness prevail in this situation and I trust You to keep me safe. Amen.

Evil – New Testament

Let him eschew evil, and do good, let him seek peace, and ensue it.

1 Peter 3: 11

Before we can eschew evil, we must define it. Adjectives for evil in the New Testament are slander, pride, deceit, maliciousness, backbiting, hatred, drunkenness, jealousy, malignity, covetousness, lust, self-willingness, idolatry, witchcraft, reveling, debate, false accusation, fierceness, and murder. Meddling with any of these traits is meddling with evil.

Jesus says evil comes from within the heart of man (Mark 7: 21-23). Demon possessed people would lose control of their bodies and endanger themselves but Christ says this kind comes out by prayer and fasting (read Matthew 17: 14-21).

The hungered Christ conquered the evil lust of the flesh when he refused Satan's offer to turn stones into bread (Matthew 4: 3). He conquered the lust for worldly power when he denied Satan's offer to rule the nations (Matthew 4: 8-10). And he conquered evil doctrine because he was a righteous man who knew no sin (1 Peter 2: 21-22; 1 John 3: 4-6).

Dear Lord, I thank You for Jesus Christ who overcomes evil. And I invite him into my heart for protection, wisdom, and salvation. Amen.

Other Bible References about Evil: Genesis 2: 9; Joshua 24: 1; Psalms 32: 13-16; Psalms 34: 21; 37: 27; Proverbs 16: 17; 28: 1; Isaiah 45: 7; Joel 2: 12-13; Matthew 5: 39; Mark 7: 21-23; Romans 12: 9; Righteousness overcomes evil: Psalms 119

Faith – Old Testament

And Joshua blessed him, and gave unto Caleb, the son of Jephunneh, Hebron, for an inheritance.
Joshua 14: 13

Caleb faithfully inherited the land he had spied out years earlier but it was not without difficulty: he was slandered and threatened with stoning for reporting the land and its inhabitants could be overcome.

We will also have troubles before receiving God's promises, but if God has ordained something, it will come true, God is not a man that he should lie; Numbers 23: 19.)

The Bible also says God's faithfulness does not fail (Psalms 89: 33). Consider reading more of God's attributes of faithfulness in the 89th Chapter of Psalms.

We are to give God the glory in all that we do and being faithful begins the journey.

Dear Lord, May I obtain the wonderful promises You have for me, by faith. Amen.

Faith – New Testament

Now faith is the substance of things hoped for, the evidence of things not seen. For by it, the elders received a good report.

Hebrews 11: 1

The practitioners of faith in God are listed in the 11th chapter of Hebrews. They obtained victories in battle, righteous decrees, and built altars for God.

But the greatest faith anyone can have is to believe in the risen Christ, who gives salvation from sin. He takes away sins by his death on the cross and arose into heaven to give people us a new life.

The Bible says, But as many as received him, to them gave he power to become sons of God, even to them that believe on his name (John 1: 12).

Christ incorporated faith works of God into his life by healing people, teaching God's word, and fellowshipping with the lost. We should be so faithful yet testify of the living Christ..

Dear Lord, Let me be faithful to complete the task You have shown me, but moreso, may I know Jesus as Savior for my life. Amen.

Other Bible References: Psalms 99; 105; 119: 89-91; John 1: 12, 13; Hebrews 12: 1-2

Fellowship – Old Testament

And Moses and Aaron went and gathered together all the elders of the children of Israel; And Aaron spoke all the words which the Lord had spoken unto Moses, and did the signs of the sight of the people.

Exodus 4: 2930

Fellowshipping with other believers makes great things happen such as when Moses, Aaron, and the elders of Israel got together and worshipped God: they made a plan to free the people from slavery.

But we can also fellowship with God when we are alone. When Moses was tending the flock near a mountain, God had appeared to him out of a burning bush, where a covenant was made.

God has said, I will be sanctified in them that come nigh me, and before all the people I will be glorified (Leviticus 10: 3).

May we consider fellowshipping with God in the congregation of believers but also personally when alone.

Dear Father in Heaven, I praise You for the brothers and sisters who have gifts of Your spirit, but also for every human – that they might find You in the midst of life and be saved from sin. Amen.

Fellowship – New Testament

And when the scribes and Pharisees saw him eat with tax collectors and sinners, they said unto his disciples, "How is it that he eateth and drinketh with tax collectors and sinners?"

Mark 2: 16

Jesus sets a wonderful example of fellowshipping when he sat down to eat with publicans, sinners, and the sick. He knew they needed to be fed God's word, so he humbled himself before them.

We should be humble in front of people with different faiths and experiences. Not only can we share our lives but give testimony of our faith in God, and we might find that we have something in common. We were once strangers to God (Ephesians 2: 19), but God had mercy to fellowship with us.

Remember, Christ said, "I came not to call the righteous, but sinners to repentance" (Luke 5: 32).

The Bible also encourages us to fellowship in the congregation of believers: "Not forsaking the assembly of ourselves together, as the manner of some is; but exhorting one another: and so much the more, as ye see the day approaching" (Hebrews. 10: 25).

Dear Lord, I thank You for my brothers and sisters all over the world. May we unite to proclaim the good news of salvation to all people. Amen.

Other Bible References: Psalms 58: 3; 133: 1; Proverbs 4: 14; 12: 11; 14: 7;; Luke 6: 32-34; Philippians 2: 1-2; Ephesians 5: 11

And Joseph said unto them, "Fear not; for am I in the place of God?"

Genesis 50: 6

Only a holy God can redeem sin but Joseph's brothers wanted Joseph to forgive them for abandoning him years earlier.

God says, "I, even I, am He who blotteth out thy transgressions for mine own sake, and will not remember sins" (Isaiah 43: 25). The Bible further confirms that forgiveness is with God (Psalms 130: 4).

However, consider reading one man's path to forgiveness: David said the sacrifices of God are a broken spirit (Psalms 51: 17). He asked for mercy, acknowledged sin, and committed himself to teach other people about God's ways.

The words given to David's son Solomon may sum up the path to finding forgiveness. "If my people, who are called by my name, shall humble themselves, and pray, and seek my face, and turn from their wicked ways, then will I hear from heaven, and will forgive their sin, and will heal their land" (2 Chronicles 7: 14).

Dear Lord, I humbly confess my sin. Please forgive me and create a new heart within me to serve You in righteousness. Amen

Forgiveness – New Testament

"And when ye stand praying, forgive, if ye have ought against any, that your Father also, who is in heaven, may forgive you your trespasses."

Mark 11: 25

Jesus says the first requirement to being personally forgiven by God of sin is to forgive all other people of sin.

However, we may have sinned against God himself by failing to put Him first in tithing, activities, and family loyalty.

For these sins to be removed, they must be completely acknowledged and put on the back on God's sinless Son, Jesus, who takes away sin. Christ Jesus is the pure sacrifice for our sins that allows us to become completely forgiven.

The Bible says, If we confess our sins, he is faithful and just to forgive us our sins, and to cleanse us from all unrighteousness (1 John 1: 9-2: 2).

Sins may take years to redeem, but we are encouraged to patiently redeem the time (Ephesians 5: 9-17).

Dear Lord, I confess my sins and abandon them. And I thank You for Christ who took my sins upon His back to the cross. Forgiveness is truly with You, and Your mercy endures forever. Amen.

Other Bible References: Psalms 25: 16-18; 86: 5-8; 130: 1-4; Romans 9: 15-18; Ephesians 1: 3-14; 4: 32

Friends – Old Testament

Now when Job's three friends heard of all this evil that was come upon him, they came every one from his own place; Eliphaz the Tenamite, and Bildad the Shuhite, and Zophar the Naamathite: for they had made an appointment together to come to mourn with him and to comfort him.

Job 2: 11

Friends came to Job's side after he suffered loss of family, farm, and health, but none could comfort him. Job said, "Miserable comforters are ye all."

Friends may always not understand our problems but God does. He instigated Job's poor condition to show His glory yet communed with him.

Consider getting to know God as a friend so when difficult times come you will have someone to trust.

For domestic friendship, the Bible says, To have friends, one must show himself friendly (Proverbs 18: 24), and a friend loves at all times (Proverbs 17: 17).

Nevertheless, we are advised never to completely trust a friend (Micah 7: 5), but in contrast there is a friend who [stays] closer than a brother (Proverbs 18: 24).

Dear Father in Heaven, Thank you for friends, but You are my true friend who is with me and I humbly seek your face for eternal companionship. Amen.

Friends – New Testament

If there be therefore any consolation in Christ, if any comfort of love, if any fellowship of the Spirit, if any bowels and mercies, Fulfill ye my joy, that ye be like-minded, having the same love, being of one accord, of one mind. Let nothing be done through strife or vainglory; but in lowliness of mind let each esteem other better than themselves.

Philippians 2: 1-3

Performing all those precepts makes many friends but we should also consider Jesus a friend.

He said, "Henceforth, I call you not servants; for the servant knoweth not what his lord doeth: but I have called you friends; for all things that I have heard of my Father I have made known unto you" (John 15: 15).

Jesus shares with us the wonderful truth from God about finding salvation.

May we think about opening our hearts to let Jesus in and be our friend. He has given the ultimate sacrifice for us by laying down his life.

Dear Lord, I humble myself before my friends to listen, encourage, and help, but may Jesus Christ may our true bond for friendship that keeps us joyful in God's Holy Spirit.

Other Bible References: Proverbs 16: 28; 27: 6; John 15: 12

Gambling – Old Testament

And Samson said unto them, "I will now put forth a riddle unto you: if ye can certainly declare it me within the seven days of the feast, and find it out, then I will give you thirty sheets and thirty change of garments."

Judges 14: 12

Samson gambled that his thirty friends couldn't solve a riddle about a honeycomb being in a lion's carcass and he lost.

Then he gambled his new wife Delilah couldn't find his strength and he lost again when a man shaved the locks of Samson's hair to weaken him.

Samson's final gamble came when he pulled down the pillars of an outdoor stadium and he lost his life, though he had asked God for permission in prayer to avenge his enemies.

Possibly we are on the losing end of a gambling spree and want to save our life. The only way we can do so is commit our ways and assets to God.

God already owns all but He expects a portion of assets to be returned to Him (Genesis 28: 22; Leviticus 27: 30-34). And He always wants our time and service.

Dear Lord, Thank You for providing me assets. May I invest them for Your purpose rather than mine, and I will be in the right place to serve You. Amen.

Gambling – New Testament

And when he had spent all, there arose a mighty famine in that land, and he began to be in want.

Luke 15: 14

Jesus tells a story about a young man going out and wasting his father's goods with riotous living and becoming famished; he wanted to return home. And his father was waiting for him with open arms.

Our Father in heaven welcomes us home when we remorsefully acknowledge wasting assets and time. He has had mercy upon thousands of people who love Him.

The wisest investment we can make is giving our life to God. We will be in the right place to receive a sure return on our investment. The peace of mind that comes from being God is a reward that is free upon our confession of sin.

Dear Lord, Thank You for providing Christ who has died for my sin. I confess my sin and promise to commit all my assets to You. Sustain me with Your provisions I pray. Amen.

Other Bible References: Matthew 25: 14-30; Luke 16: 1-31; 19: 19-26; Timothy 6: 18

Humble – Old Testament

And thou shalt remember all the way the Lord thy God led thee this forty years in the wilderness, to humble, and to prove thee, to know what was in thine heart, whether thou wouldest keep his commandments or not.

Deuteronomy 8: 2

God will humble us in life as he did the Israelites in the wilderness to know He is God.

Either we submit to His authority or continue in prideful ways to destruction. Moses scorned the people for their stubbornness and disobedience (Deuteronomy 9).

Consider beginning each day humbly in prayer to God, for the Bible says, Humility is life (Proverbs 22: 4).

The writer of Psalms 69 was humbled: poor, sorrowful, reproached by enemies. drowning in waters, hated, ashamed, and with no friends, yet he praised God with a song and gave thanks (Psalms 69: 30).

The humble shall see this and be glad; and your heart shall live that seek God (Palms 69: 32).

Dear Lord, My heart is not haughty, nor mine eyes lofty: neither do I exercise myself in great matters, or in things too high for me. Surely I have behaved and quieted myself, as a child that is weaned of his mother: my soul is even as a weaned child; (Psalms 131). Amen.

67

Humble – New Testament

Whosoever, therefore, shall humble himself as the little child, the same is greatest in the kingdom of heaven.

Matthew 18: 4

Being humble means to lower oneself. Pride has been abandoned. Selfish desires are gone. And there is a willingness to serve God and man.

Humility also receives correction. The Bible says this correction allows us to partake of God's holiness and yields the peaceable fruits of righteousness (Hebrews 12: 8-11).

If you have a problem being humble, consider fasting from food periodically to know God alone can meet your needs. Consider listening more than speaking.

Jesus quietly listened to problems and humbled himself before man and God/

Humility is a virtue that protects us, for the Bible says that God gives grace to the humble (1 Peter 5: 5).

Dear God, Humble me to be more like Jesus, who served the people's needs and was obedient to You. Amen.

Other Bible References: Matthew 5: 5; 18: 3; Luke 14: 11; Philippians 2: 8; Hebrews 12: 2

Imprisonment – Old Testament

And Joseph's master took him and put him into the prison, a place where the king's prisoners were bound: and he was there in the prison.

Genesis 39: 20

Joseph was falsely accused by his master's wife of seduction and put into prison but Joseph kept his faith in God to become free.

Imprisonment is a terrible, lonely experience, but God is still there for anyone who calls on His name.

Psalms 145 and 146 inspires a prisoner to hope in the living God.

When the ruler Pharaoh wanted a dream interpreted rightfully, he called for the faithful man Joseph and freed him from prison.

The Lord upholdeth all that fall, and raiseth up all those who are bowed down (Psalms 145: 14). He has the power to free the prisoners (Psalms 146: 7).

Dear Father in Heaven, This jail is dreadful, yet I know You have the power to give me freedom. I call upon Your name Lord in truth, mercy, and faith to protect and have mercy on me. Amen.

69

Imprisonment – New Testament

"Are they ministers of Christ? (I speak as a fool) I am more: in labors more abundant, in stripes above measure, in prisons more frequently, in deaths often."

2 Corinthians 11: 23

The Apostle Paul was a prisoner for Christ's sake but many of us are prisoners because we disobeyed the law; however, the law is our schoolmaster that brings us to know Christ, according to scripture (Galatians 3: 24).

Being in prison is a good time for thinking about what we have done to get there and repenting of the crime.

Christ said he came "to preach deliverance to the captives and set at liberty those who are bruised" (Luke 4: 18). Christ Jesus has passed through the veil of darkness to give us access to God and light upon our confession of sin (Hebrews 6: 18: 19). Acceptance of Christ turns our lives around.

Experiencing this new birth and freedom in Christ makes us want to tell others. The Apostle Paul shared the gospel of salvation with a keeper of the prison, and he became saved (Acts 16: 19).

Dear Father in Heaven, Protect me I pray. I Thank You for Your wonderful word of life. You give me hope and Christ Jesus is a friend I can trust. Amen.

Other Bible References: Luke 23: 43; John 8: 36; Romans 8: 2; Galatians 3: 25; 5: 1; Philippians 2: 8

Jealousy – Old Testament

And Saul eyed David, from that day and forward.
1 Samuel 18: 9

Saul became jealous of David after David killed the giant Goliath and became a hero among the people. David was also good looking and loved by his family.

But if we know God, we should not become jealous of anyone or anything: it is God whom we love first in obedience to His First Commandment.

But God does have a right to be jealous. He becomes jealous of us when we worship anything or anyone other than Him (Deuteronomy 32: 21); and He will correct us to know He is God.

We don't want to become the objects of someone's vengeance prayer like David's but we want to draw close to God in devotion and love.

Dear Lord, I abandon jealousy of other people to worship You in my life. I am content to serve You in righteousness and truth. Amen.

Jealousy – New Testament

Let us not be desirous of vain glory, provoking one another, envying one another.

Galatians 5: 26

Envying another person takes time away from worshipping God.

Our focus should be on God's Son Jesus conforming more to the image of this heavenly Savior who is able to intercede for us (Romans 8: 29; 12: 1-16).

The Bible says, If ye then be risen with Christ, seek those things which are above, where Christ sitteth on the right hand of God. Set your affection on things above, not on things on the earth (Colossians 3: 1-2).

Consider Christ who took on himself no reputation, worldly title, expensive clothes, or personal assets but was received by God as Son. Each of us who confesses Christ is received by God and we have a unique gift of the spirit (1 Corinthians 12: 11).

Dear Lord, Humble me before You so that I am not envious of anyone of anything. You are my life, and I thank you for my friends in Christ Jesus. Amen.

Other Bible References about Jealousy: Proverbs 3: 31; 6: 34; 14: 30; 23: 17; 27: 4; 1 Corinthians 13: 4; Romans 13: 13; James 3: 17-18; 4: 5-6

Joyfulness – Old Testament

And he will love thee, and bless thee, and multiply thee; he will also bless the fruit of thy womb, and the fruit of thy land . . . .
Deuteronomy 7: 13

Happiness may be defined as the freedom to do as we please but with God in the Old Testament happiness is defined as obeying His laws and loving Him with all thine heart, mind, soul, and strength (Deuteronomy 6-8; 28: 1-14).

But there will be troubles to pursuing happiness: sickness, enemies, sin, or hunger will take place. God puts these obstacles in our path to strengthen our faith in Him.

Knowing God has power over these troubles keeps us in the right place to be joyful.

The writer of The Book of Ecclesiastes considers the subject of happiness and says: There is nothing better for a man, than that he should eat and drink, and that he should make his soul enjoy the good of all his labor (Ecclesiastes 2: 24). Solomon summarizes his dissertation and says, Fear God and keep His commandments: for this is the whole duty of man (Ecclesiastes 12: 13).

Consider acknowledging God in your life and following His plan for happiness. Our plans are doomed to fail but God's plan has proved to work despite the hardships.

Dear Lord, I thank You for being here. Your joy is truly my strength. I confess my sins and free my mind to work and glorify You. Amen.

Joyfulness – New Testament

And the angel said unto them, "Fear not: for, behold, I bring you good tidings of great joy, which shall be to all people."

Luke 2: 10

The shepherds became joyful when they heard the good news of Christ's birth, so they immediately went to Bethlehem to see the child. Upon seeing the Savior, they returned home praising and glorifying God.

The righteous man, Simeon, who had waited long for the consolation of Israel was also joyful as he held the baby in his arms and blessed God. And Christ's mother, Mary, said a lengthy prayer that praised God.

Christ is a risen Savior who frees us from sin and allows us to enter the joy of our Father in heaven. He was born for our salvation and it gives us happiness to know him.

Dear Father in Heaven, It was for joy Jesus was born to take away sin. Thank You for releasing me of sin to have pure joy on earth. Amen.

Other Bible References: Job 41: 22; Psalms 16: 11; 51: 12; Proverbs 14: 10; Lamentations 2: 15; Luke 15: 7; John 3: 29; Philippians 2: 12; 1 Peter 1: 8

Loneliness –Old Testament

And the Lord God said, "It is not good that the man should be alone: I will make him a help meet for him."

Genesis 2: 18

Loneliness is the primary reason why God created a woman to be with man, but some people are called to be separated to the Lord, such as the Nazarene, who vowed a vow of separation to God (Numbers 6).

Also, a eunuch was encouraged to not think they he was a dry tree, but the Lord says they have a place within his walls and house (Isaiah 56: 3-5).

During a feeling of loneliness, consider fellowshipping with God but also with other believers.

The Bible says, Bless ye God in the congregations, even the Lord, from the fountain of Israel (Psalms 68: 26).

Dear Lord, This loneliness is a good time to learn more about You. I praise You for Your presence here and I thank You for other believers who worship in the world. Amen.

Loneliness – New Testament

. . . I will never leave thee, nor forsake thee.

Hebrews 13: 5

The 13th Chapter of Hebrews affirms that God is with us but we are encouraged to entertain strangers, remember those who are afflicted, endorse marriage, pray for those in authority, be subject to religious leaders, and worship in the congregation.

But Jesus treasured his time alone: he went to the desert, mountain, and garden to pray to God. And once when he was with his disciples, he went off a short distance to fellowship with God.

Pleasing God helps us to know that we are not alone. He told Jesus, "This is my beloved Son, in whom I am well pleased" (Matthew 17: 5).

But if we are not pleasing God, we are indeed alone (Romans 8: 5-8). We are like the branches without a vine as Jesus describes in St. John 15: 1-11.

But with Jesus, who is like the vine, we become nourished and the pathway to God is open (John 14: 23). And the Holy Spirit resides with us (John 15: 26).

Dear Lord, I praise You for being here in my loneliness, and I thank You for Jesus who died for my sin. May my loneliness be turned into companionship with You and others who praise Your Holy Name. Amen.

Other Bible References about Loneliness: Joshua 1: 9; Psalms 18:6; 68: 5-6; 133: 1; Matthew 5: 16; Romans 10: 13, 20; I John 1: 3

Lost – Old Testament

Now for a long season, Israel hat been without the true God, and without a teaching priest, and without law.

2 Chronicles 15: 3

The people of Israel were spiritually lost: there was no peace in the land, nation destroyed nation, city destroyed city, and great vexations occurred. So God sent Azania the prophet to meet Asa, King of Israel and said, "The Lord is with you while you are with him; and if ye seek him, he will be found by you . . ." (verse 2).

Establishing a covenant of God begins a journey to become found and have peace.

King Asa put away all the golden images and abominable idols that were defiling the land and people, and he renewed the altar of the Lord. The people returned to the law of God with all their heart and soul.

The Bible says, Blessed is the man that walketh not in the counsel of the ungodly, nor standeth in the way of sinners, nor sitteth in the seat of the scornful. But his delight is in the law of the Lord . . . he shall be like a tree planted by the rivers of water . . . (Psalms 1: 1).

The tree remains in its place of nourishment, as we who keep the word of God.

Dear Lord, I praise You for Your presence here in stillness. You are my home and I am found by You in belief and faith. Grant me peace, rest, and happiness. Amen.

77

Lost – New Testament

For the Son of Man is come to save that which was lost.
Matthew 18: 11

Jesus is able to save the lost because he can remove sins.

But the Bible says many people have fallen victim to false doctrine and are led astray -- that some shall depart from the faith, giving heed to seducing spirits, and doctrines of devils (1 Timothy 4: 1).

When you feel lost, consider humbling yourself and seeking God with your whole heart. God is an anchor for the soul (Hebrews 6: 19). And Christ commands us to love the Lord thy God with all thy heart, and with all thy soul, and with all thy mind, and with all thy strength – and thy neighbor as thyself (Mark 12: 30-31).

Obeying Christ's sermon on the mount keeps us in the right attitude: "Blessed are the poor in spirit: for theirs is the kingdom of heaven . . . " (Matthew 5: 1-12).

Dear Lord, Life is so confusing, but I trust You to lead me safely and righteously. May I have peace, rest, and happiness. Amen.

Other Bible References: Psalms 119: 176; Proverbs 4: 20-27; Isaiah 48: 17; 55: 6; Matthew 10: 39; Romans 10: 20; Ephesians 4: 14-15

Love – Old Testament

"Where thou diest, will I die, and there will I be buried; the Lord do so to me, and more also if anything but death part thee and me."

Ruth 1: 17

Ruth gives a wonderful example of love for her mother-in-law when she vows to stay by her side until death. (Naomi was heartbroken because her two sons had died and she wanted to return to her homeland.)

Our love should be so strong, but our first love should be for God.

The Bible commands, And thou shalt love the Lord thy God with all thine heart, and with all thy soul, and with all thy might (Deuteronomy 6: 5).

But expressing God's love for others testifies of our faith (Leviticus 19: 18). Ruth invoked God's name as the guarantor of her promise and she was rewarded with rest and safety.

Dear Lord, I love You with all my heart, mind, soul, and strength. May I set an example of love towards others with humble service that glorifies You and produces good work in mercy. Amen.

Love – New Testament

Charity suffereth long, and is kind; charity envieth not; charity vaunteth not itself, is not puffed up . . . .

1 Corinthians 13: 4-8

Before we can express love, we need to define its sixteen characteristics in the scriptures.

Love is patient. Love is kind. Love is not envious. Love is not vain. Love is not puffed up. Love does not behave itself indecently. Love does not pursue its own things. Love is not easily provoked. Love thinks no evil. Love does not rejoice over wrong. Love rejoices with the truth. Love quietly covers all things. Love believes all things. Love hopes all things. Love endures all things. Love never fails.

Quietly think about each item and how to apply it towards other people.

But Christ has expressed the greatest love when he gave up his life for our sins (John 15: 13). We are free to serve the living God and share the news with other people.

Christ summarizes the attitude we should have towards others when he said, "that ye love one another, as I have loved you" (John 15: 12).

Dear God, I praise You for Jesus, who provides me the path to love you more. Amen.

Other Bible References: Deuteronomy 6: 5; Proverbs 8: 17; 15: 9; Hosea 14: 4; John 3: 16; 13: 34; 14: 21; 15: 13; Romans 5: 8; 1 John 4; 7, 16-19

Lying – Old Testament

And Jacob said unto his father, "I am Esau, thy first-born; I have done according to thou badest me: arise, I pray thee, sit and eat of my venison, that thy soul may bless me."

Genesis 27: 19

Jacob lied to his nearly blind father about being Esau so he would get his older brother's blessing.

We may lie to get something we want or try to be something we aren't, but God will confront our lies, because He loves us enough to correct us.

He confronted Jacob'in a private place where an angel wrestled Jacob to the ground and wounded his thigh.

God forbid it takes an injury before we tell the truth but usually something bad happens before we admit truth (read more about God confronting lies: Psalms 50: 16-23; 90: 8).

The Bible says, Thou shalt not bear false witness against thy neighbor (Exodus 20: 16); and thou shalt not raise a false report (Exodus 23: 1).

Dear Lord, Forgive me for lying and have mercy on me. May I tell the truth from now on. May my apology be accepted. Amen.

Lying – New Testament

But Peter said, "Ananias, why hath Satan filled thine heart to lie to the Holy Ghost, and to keep back part of the price of the land?"
Acts 5: 3

Apostle Ananias lied to other apostles about his wealth being put in the common treasury, and when Ananias was confronted by the Holy Spirit, he was struck dead (Acts 5: 1-5).

Lying always hurts someone, whether it be the liar or the victim of the lie.

Rather than face God's harsh judgment, we should privately come to the truth right now: we are sinners who need Christ Jesus (Ephesians 4: 21-29). He can help us face who we are, what we are, and where we're going, but we must yield to God's righteous desire for our lives and consider Christ as a sacrifice for sins.

The Bible says, Wherefore putting away lying, speak every man truth with his neighbor; for we are members one of another (Ephesians 4: 25).

Consider also reading Colossians 3: 5-17 for living a life of truth.

Dear Father in Heaven, Forgive me for lying, and help me confess the truth. I praise You for Jesus who died for my sin to let me live in truth. Amen.

Other Bible References: Exodus 23: 1; Numbers 23: 19; Psalms 15: 1-3; 31: 18; 51: 6; 119: 163; 145: 18; Proverbs 12: 19; 21: 23; Isaiah 63: 8; Zechariah 8: 16; Matthew 12: 18, 36; John 3: 32; Ephesians 2: 4; Hebrews 6: 18; 1 Peter 3: 10; I John 1: 8-10; 2: 22-29; Revelation 21: 8; Psalm 120: Deliverance from lying lips

Marriage – Old Testament

And Abraham said unto his eldest servant of his house that ruled over all that he had, "Put, I pray thee, thy hand under my thigh; and I will make thee swear by the Lord, the God of heavens, and the God of all the earth, that thou shalt not take a wife unto my son of the daughters of the Canaanites, among whom I dwell."

Genesis 24: 2-3

Abraham's son Isaac was sad because his mother had died, so father Abraham sent out a servant to find a wife for Isaac in a land of God's own people.

Finding a mate among God's people eliminates a lot of problems, because there is an agreement that God is the first priority for life.

When the servant arrived, he sat by a well of water where Rebekah arrived and offered the servant and his animals water to drink. The servant took this as a sign from God that the kind woman Rebekah would be a bride for Isaac.

As men, we might look among God's people for a kind woman, and women might be kind to strangers who know the Lord and introduce them to family.

But the most important thing is to know God. Rebekah and Isaac spoke of God and were committed to Him, and they married.

Dear Lord, I look to You for the right mate in my life, but first I want to make sure my own spiritual house is in order. Forgive my sin and bring me into a right relationship with You. Amen.

Marriage – New Testament

Wives, submit, yourselves unto your own husbands, as unto the Lord. For the husband is the head of the wife, even as Christ is the head of the church: and he is the savior of the body . . . Husbands, love your wives, even as Christ also loved the church, and gave himself for it.

Ephesians 5: 22-25

Christ is the true bond for marriage because he takes away sin, intercedes for us in prayer, and provides a path to oneness in God.

When there is disagreement, look to Christ for agreement. Where there is fault, forgive one another, as God in His abundant mercy, has forgiven us through Christ (Ephesians 4: 32).

Finally, be ye all of one mind, having compassion one of another; love as brethren, be pitiful, be courteous (1 Peter 3: 8). (Consider reading the full text of Peter's advice for married couples in 1 Peter 3: 1-12.)

Marriage is honorable in all, and the bed becomes undefiled (Hebrews 13: 4).

Dear Lord, I praise You for this marriage. May our lives be of grace, peace, righteousness, love, mercy, and happiness in Jesus. Amen.

Other Bible References about Marriage: Genesis 1: 17; 2: 18; Matthew 19: 4-6; Ephesians 5: 22-33; Colossians 3: 18-19; Redemptive laws for husband and wife: Numbers 30

Mercy – Old Testament

The Lord is merciful and gracious, slow to anger, and plenteous in mercy.

Psalms 103: 8

There are ten traits of God's mercy in Psalms 103.

The Lord forgives sins, heals diseases, redeems life from destruction, covers with love and tenderness, and puts good words in our mouths. Our youth is renewed. There is righteousness and judgment for the oppressed. Mercy is higher than the heavens; sin is removed forever; and mercy is everlasting.

How wonderful is to know we can enjoy all these mercies!

But they are dependent on a few items: reverential fear of God (verse 17), keeping His covenant, and performing His commandments (verse 18).

God's mercy endures forever for those people who love Him.

Dear Father in Heaven, Thank you for providing these mercies for all of us. May each of us depend on Your Word for life and obey Your commandments. Amen.

Mercy – New Testament

"Blessed are the merciful, for they shall obtain mercy."
Matthew 5: 7

Jesus teaches that if we show mercy to others, we will receive mercy; so we should be performing merciful acts such as acquiring something for someone who is in need, nursing the sick, or forgiving debts.

Christ gives us a good illustration of mercy when he shared a story about a stranger who had fell among thieves and was beaten. A good Samaritan bound up the man's wounds, housed him, and gave money for his care..

Well, God is merciful to us as sinners to provide Jesus as a sacrifice for our sins (Hebrews 10: 28). And we should sacrifice part of our lives and show mercy to others to exemplify Christ's love to the world.

Dear Father in Heaven, I thank You for Jesus who took my sins to the cross to give me rest. May I tell others about Your mercy that is available upon confession of sin and repentance. Amen.

Other Bible References about Mercy: 2 Chronicles 7: 14; Psalms 25: 16-18; 116: 1-7; Proverbs 3: 3; 21: 21; 28: 13; Micah 6: 8; Matthew 5: 7; Luke 6: 36; Ephesians 2: 4-5; Hebrews 12: 11

Money – Old Testament

And if thy way be too long for thee, so that thou art not able to carry it . . . then shalt thou turn it into money, and bind up the money in thine hand, and shalt go unto the place which the Lord thy God shall choose.

Deuteronomy 14: 24-25

Money is a component God incorporated to lessen our load, not make it heavier. If we have some extra, we should increase tithes to the Lord, invest in the market (for His glory), or distribute liberally to the poor.

What we are not to do is hoard money, for the Bible says, There is a sore evil which I have seen under the sun, namely, riches kept for the owners thereof to their hurt. But those riches perish by evil travail . . . (Ecclesiastes 5: 13-14).

Our desire should be as King Solomon, who did not ask God for riches or wealth but asked God for wisdom and understanding -- and God blessed him with material wealth (2 Chronicles 1: 11-12). That proves seeking God's will in life supplies necessary provisions.

Dear Lord, I put You first in my life and I trust You to supply my needs. May my assets be invested to extend Your kingdom. Amen.

Money – New Testament

. . . Ye cannot serve God and [money].

Matthew 6: 24

Serving God performs good works, proclaims His word, and administers gifts of the Holy Spirit but serving a desire for money only leads to more work, anxiety, and disappointment.

A rich man questioned Jesus about how to live a long life and Jesus told him to sell what he had, distribute to the poor, and follow him (Luke 18: 18-22).

Jesus advises us to lay not up for ourselves treasures on earth but in heaven, where moth nor rust corrupts, and thieves can not steal: for where our treasure is, there will our heart be also (Matthew 6: 19-21).

Serving God should be our priority in life -- and Jesus says all other things shall be added unto us (Matthew 6: 26-33).

Consider beginning each day with a righteous heart and mind towards serving God:

He is a rewarder to those that believe in Him (Hebrews 11: 6).

Dear Father in Heaven, You are my first desire in life, and I commit my ways to You. Thank You for providing my riches in Christ Jesus and my daily bread. Amen.

Other Bible References about Money: Psalms 49: 6-20; Proverbs 3: 9-10; 28-20; 30: 8-9; Isaiah 55: 1; Mark 10: 23-25; 12: 4; Luke 12: 33-34; 18: 22; 19: 23; Philippians 4: 19: 1 Timothy. 6: 10-18; James 5: 1-6

Obedience – Old Testament

Now the word of the Lord came unto Jonah, the son of Amittai, saying, "Arise, go to Nineveh, that great city, and cry against it: for their wickedness is come up before me," but Jonah rose up to flee unto Tarshish from the presence of the Lord.

Jonah 1: 1-3

Jonah knew where he was supposed to go and what he was supposed to do but he went the opposite way.

That's what we do sometimes: the Lord wants us to go somewhere and do something but we go the opposite way.

Jonah found himself in the middle of a big storm on a sinking boat with an angry crew for disobeying God's command to go and preach to the city of Nineveh. The crew then decided to get rid of him by sending him into the water.

The Bible says obedience is better than sacrifice (1 Samuel 15: 22).

Though God loves whom He corrects, we do not want to be cast overboard like Jonah who was swallowed up by a whale and spit upon on a beach.

Dear Lord, It is difficult to obey, but I choose to be humble and obedient. Bless me Lord as I faithfully endure Your word for life. Amen.

Obedience – New Testament

And being found in fashion as a man, he humbled himself and became obedient, unto death, even the death of the cross.
Philippians 2: 8

God's son, Christ, sets a wonderful example of obedience when he received a command to die for the people's sins and walked to the court of judgment to be sentenced to death and hung on a tree post.

Though our purpose is to live and proclaim the good news of the sacrificial death of Christ, we should do so without complaining – knowing God has also reserved something in heaven better for us as believers (Hebrews 12: 2).

The Apostles affirmed that God is the ultimate benefactor for life, and they adjured to God's will rather than man's (Acts 5: 9). Our final accountability is to God (Romans 14: 11-12).

Nevertheless, we are to obey those who have the rule over us (Hebrews 13: 17), that we might also obtain a good report.

Dear Father in Heaven, Christ's obedience inspires me to follow Your calling and do it with joy, knowing that I too will be delivered into something better. May I indeed fulfill the mission of presenting Christ as Savior to the world. Amen.

Other Bible References: Exodus 19: 5; 24: 7; Deuteronomy 4—8; 2 Corinthians 2: 9

Patience – Old Testament

And Jacob served seven years for Rachel: and they seemed unto him but a few days, for the love he had to her.

Genesis 29: 20

Jacob waited fourteen years for Rachel because Uncle Laban deceitfully gave Leah for him to marry.

Jacob had lots of patience waiting for the one he loved but he didn't sit idle: he multiplied his cattle to become rich.

While being patient for thing to happen that God has ordained, we can get busy on something else that gives God glory.

The Bible encourages to be patient during troubled times: "My soul, wait thou upon God; for my expectation is from Him," (Psalm 62: 5).

We are to trust God for all things (Psalms 37). What we are not to do is hasten after and serve another god (Psalms 16: 4).

Dear Lord, Your patience is infinite and Your understanding forever. While I wait for Your promise of eternal joy, I will continue to work for Your glory. Amen.

Patience – New Testament

For ye have need of patience, that, after ye have done the will of God, ye might receive the promise.

Hebrews 10: 36

The promises that we receive upon belief in Christ are redemption from sins and being able to rest one day from our labors, Until that time, we are encouraged to endure suffering and life with patience (James 5: 7-18; 1 Peter 2: 20).

The Bible further says, Troubles works patience (Romans 5: 3); the trying of our faith worketh patience (James 1: 3); and we are to let patience have her perfect work (James 1: 4).

Jesus was mocked, scourged, and crucified, yet he patiently focused on being with his Father in Heaven.

Consider reading the Book of James to strengthen your patience.

Jesus also said, "In your patience possess ye your souls" (Luke 21: 19).

Dear Lord, Your patience is everlasting and I wait upon you to receive the promise. May I be productive for Your sake. Amen.

Other Bible References about Patience: Psalms 23: 14; 37: 7; 40: 1; Proverbs 25: 8; Ecclesiastes 7: 8; Matthew 24: 13; Luke 8: 15; 21: 19; James 1: 2-4; 5: 7-8; 1 Peter 2: 20

Peace – Old Testament

And there was a strife between the headsmen of Abram's cattle and the herdsmen of Lot's cattle: and the Canaanite and Perizzite dwelt then in the land.

Genesis 13: 7

Abram and Lot's herdsmen were about to fight over grazing land for their animals, so Abram called a meeting and the two men met at an intersection overlooking a vast amount of land and came to an agreement: Lot would occupy one part of the land and Abraham the other. But it was Abram who first yielded by letting Lot choose first.

When there is a disagreement with someone, we should consider yielding to the other person. It may mean God has something better for us.

Lot had chosen the plain of Jordan but the men of those cities were wicked and Lot was taken captive.

If there is no peace in our personal lives, then we should obviously yield to God who has power over our lives and gives us peace by the confession of sin and repentance from evil.

Setting our hearts and mind on God puts in the right place to receive peace.

Dear Lord, I humble myself from fighting and arguing, and I seek the peace that comes from You. The battle is yours Lord. Amen.

93

Peace – New Testament

Therefore, being justified by faith, we have peace with God through our Lord Jesus Christ.

Romans 5: 1

Jesus is able to give us peace because he can take away sin, but many of us think peace is at a quiet beach, desert, or a mountain stream. While these places give us physical peace by the absence of sound, true peace comes by agreement with God through Jesus.

A man, who was cutting himself and could not be restrained was found sitting in his right mind after he met and worshipped Jesus (Mark 5: 1-20).

But domestically, Jesus did not come to bring peace but division (Luke 12: 51-53) – knowing his new testament would separate the people.

Yet the Apostle Paul said that Jesus has established peace -- by breaking down the middle wall of partition between those of different beliefs (Ephesians 2: 13-16).

Dear Lord, I am comfortable knowing You are here with me to give me peace through Jesus. I accept Jesus into my heart and I will be at peace with all people. Amen.

Other Bible References about Peace: Leviticus 26: 6; Job 34: 29-30; Psalms 4: 8; 34: 14; 119: 165; Proverbs 16: 7; 17: 1; Ecclesiastes 4: 6; Isaiah 26: 3; 30: 5; Matthew 5: 9; John 14: 27; Philippians 4: 7; Colossians 3: 15; Hebrews 12: 14; 1 Peter 3: 11

Persecution – Old Testament

And the officers of the children of Israel, whom Pharaoh's task makers had set over them, were beaten . . . .

Exodus 5: 14

The officers were beaten because their subordinates could not keep up with a workload Pharaoh kept increasing -- to hinder the Hebrew people from finding time to go to the wilderness to worship their God.

Persecutors may increase our workload, defame us, or even try to kill us, but God is going to get His glory as He saved the Hebrews and drowned the pursuing Egyptian army in the sea.

Our accountability is to be faithful to God (Deuteronomy 4: 14-20). God is the one who has created us and willingly accepts us upon death if we have pleased Him.

Know that our suffering is for Him and will inspire others to find the salvation and peace that comes from God by our actions of faith.

Dear Lord, "O Lord my God, in thee do I put my trust; save me from all those who persecute me, and deliver me;" Psalm 7: 1. Amen.

Yea, and all that will live godly in Christ Jesus shall suffer persecution.

2 Timothy 3: 12

Living godly in Christ Jesus exposes believers to persecution because the devil loves to afflict meek and humble people. But Christians have Jesus as an intercessor, and the Holy Spirit as Comforter.

The devout Christian Stephen, who was accused of subverting the law and slandering Moses, looked up to see Jesus sitting on the right hand of God (Acts 6: 9-7: 60).

When persecutions, slander, threatenings, and afflictions come, confront the devil with the truth from God and the spiritual power of Jesus.

However, we are to be blameless, such as the archangel Michael who did not accuse Satan but said, "The Lord rebukes thee" (Jude 1: 9).

We are warned to resist the devil and be steadfast in the faith (1 Peter 5: 9). And we are encouraged to be strong in the Lord, and in the power of His might (Ephesians 6: 10).

Prayer of Jesus: "But I say unto you, Love your enemies, bless them that curse you, do good to them that hate you, and pray for them which despitefully use you, and persecute you" (Matthew 5: 44).

Other Bible References about Persecution: Psalms 7: 1-2; 9: 9; 91: 3; Proverbs 24: 15-16; John 6: 15; 16: 13; Romans 8: 36-37; 1 Corinthians 4: 11-13; 2 Corinthians 4: 8-11; Philippians 1: 28-30; 2 Timothy 3: 12; James 5: 16; Hebrews. 11: 37-40; 1 Peter 4: 19

Prayer – Old Testament

Now when Daniel knew that the writing was signed, he went into his house, and his windows being open in his chamber toward Jerusalem, he kneeled upon his knees three times a day, and prayed and gave thanks before his God, as he did aforetime.

Daniel 6: 10

King Darius had signed a decree for all men to come to him when they needed something, but Daniel knew God alone would furnish his needs, and so he prayed towards God's holy temple.

The temple is open to us but we must humble ourselves and seek the Lord.

The prophet Isaiah said, For the Lord is our Judge, the Lord is our lawgiver, the Lord is our king; he will save us (Isaiah 33: 22). Devotion to prayer reminds us of God sovereignty and righteous statutes over our lives.

The prayerful man David said, "Evening, and morning, and at noon, will I pray, and cry aloud, and he shall hear my voice" (Psalms 55: 17).

God hears the prayer of the righteous (Proverbs 15: 29), but He will not hear a prayer of iniquity (Psalms 66: 18).

May we set aside time to be with God in prayer.

Dear Lord, I close my eyes and pour out my emotions to You. Bless me Lord as I listen to Your guidance for my life. Amen.

Prayer – New Testament

But thou, when thou prayest, enter into thy closet, and when thou hast shut thy door, pray to thy Father, who is in secret; and thy Father, who seeth in secret, shall reward thee openly.

Matthew 6: 6

Going into a closed room and being able to commune with the almighty God through Jesus Christ is the greatest gift ever given to man. When troubles come, God is here to fix them. When sickness comes, God is here to heal. When evil comes, God is here with righteousness for victory. When there's a temptation to sin, God is here with Jesus to help us overcome and extinguish sin.

Divine prayer closes the eyes, addresses God, and listens. The Bible says, Wherefore, my beloved brethren, let every man be swift to hear, slow to speak, slow to wrath (James 1: 19). For we know not what we should pray for as we ought; but the Spirit itself maketh intercession for us with groanings which cannot be uttered (Romans 8: 26).

Jesus gives us good examples of intimate prayer with God in John 14-17. But there are times to personally petition God for help in prayer, and Jesus exhorts us saying, "And all things, whatever ye shall ask in prayer, believing, ye shall receive" (Matthew 21: 22).

Dear Father in Heaven, I love you and I thank you for the sacrifice of Jesus who allows me to commune with You in prayer. Amen.

Other Bible References about Prayer: 2 Chronicles 7: 14-15; Psalms 5: 1-3; 10: 17; 65: 1-2; 66: 18; 119: 164; Proverbs 15: 29; 28: 9; Isaiah 55: 11; Matthew 6: 1-13; Mark 1: 24; Luke 18: 1; Ephesians 3: 20; 1 Thessalonians 5: 17; Philippians 4: 6; 1 John 5: 14-15; Revelation 3: 20

Pride – Old Testament

The king spoke, and said, "Is not this great Babylon, that I have built for the house of thy kingdom by the might of my power, and for the honor of my majesty?"

Daniel 4: 30

Nebuchadnezzar proudly exclaimed he had built his kingdom by his power, but as he spoke, a voice came from heaven telling him that his kingdom would be cut down:

When our pride gets high like Nebuchadnezzar, God will humble us. The Bible says, Pride goeth before destruction, and a haughty spirit before a fall (Proverbs 16: 18).

Nebuchadnezzar was driven to live with the beasts of the fields, but after being humbled, Nebuchadnezzar praised and declared God was just and truthful.

May we acknowledge the rule and glory of God.

"Nor by might, and not by power, but by my spirit, saith the Lord" (Zech. 4: 6).

Dear Lord, Forgive me for being so prideful, and humble me to know You better. Amen.

Pride – New Testament

Be of the same mind toward one another. Mind not high things, but condescend to men of low estate. Be not wise in your own conceits.

Romans 3: 16

The Bible further says, For all that is in the world, the lust of the flesh, and the lust of the eyes, and the pride of life; is not of the Father, but is of the world. And the world passeth away and the lust of it: but he that doeth the will of God abideth forever (1 John 2: 16-17).

Abandoning pride gives us rest. We do not have to prove anything to anyone, nor strive to be something we aren't. We are simply to rest in the Lord and obeys His commandments.

The Bible also says, Let nothing be done through strife or vain glory . . . .(Philippians 2: 3).

The Apostle Paul encourages us to walk worthy of the vocation we are called, with all lowliness and meekness, with long-suffering, forbearing one another in love (Ephesians 4: 1-2).

Dear Father in Heaven, I abandon selfish pride to be humble and serve You. Amen.

Other Bible References about Pride: Leviticus 26: 14-20; Deuteronomy 8: 2; Proverbs 11: 2; 16: 18; 27: 2; Psalms 101: 5; Habakkuk 2: 4; Micah 6: 8; Matthew 18: 4; Luke 14: 11; 18: 14; Philippians 2: 1-8; 1 Timothy 2: 24; James 4: 7; 1 Peter 5: 6; 1 John 2: 16

Purpose – Old Testament

And, behold, I purpose to build a house unto the name of the Lord my God, as the Lord spake unto David my father, saying, Thy son, whom I will set upon they throne in thy room, he shall build a house unto my name.

1 Kings 5: 5

One purpose for Solomon was to build a temple where people could worship; so Solomon hired the craftsmen, acquired the materials, and built the structure.

Fulfilling God's purpose gives us great joy, because we are pleasing the very God who created us.

After construction was finished, a great feast was enjoyed and a sermon was preached that glorified God (1 Kings 8: 12-66).

But fulfilling *our own* purpose will lead to a spiritual void: King Solomon's heart was later turned away from God because he had a consortium of concubines.

The Bible says, Blessed is the man whom thou choosest, and causeth to approach unto thee . . .(Psalms 65: 4).

May we listen to God's call to perform His purpose. Our lives will joyful complete knowing we are pleasing the living God.

Dear Lord, I thank You for drawing me closer to finding Your purpose for my life and experiencing the joy of serving You. Amen.

Purpose – New Testament

"Ye have not chosen me, but I have chosen you, and ordained you, that ye should go and bring forth fruit, and that your fruit should remain . . . ."

John 15: 16

Jesus chose his disciples as God chooses us for particular jobs -- but salvation from sin is the first purpose God wants for us.

Upon receiving salvation, we are free to perform God's will by extending His kingdom on earth, glorifying His name, and testifying of good works.

Jesus gives us a good example of fulfilling God's purpose: "And he that sent me is with me. The Father hath not let me alone; for I do always those things that please him (John 8: 29).

Pleasing God fulfills purpose. When life seems vain, look for God's purpose by becoming humble and willing to serve.

He reveals His purpose in prayer (read Ephesians 1: 3-9).

Dear Lord, I thank You for showing me the purpose for life. May I share with others the saving power of Jesus in the Holy Spirit. Amen.

Other Bible References: Proverbs 20: 18; Isaiah 46: 11; Romans 8: 28; 9: 14-23; Ephesians 3: 11; 5: 9

Rejected – Old Testament

The stone which the builders refused is become the head stone of the corner. This is the Lord's doing; it is marvelous in our eyes.

Psalms 118: 22

Stone builders often throw back a stone because it does not fit in the straight line of a wall, but when the builders get to the corner, it fits.

Life can be like that. We get rejected from some common job yet know we produce good work.

Being rejected is a good time to refine talents and increase faith in the Lord. If we are patient enough, we will be called for something better.

May we humbly accept the rejection that comes from the world but willingly the acceptance from God.

Dear Lord, Though I have been rejected, I know You accept me. I humbly bow before You and trust You. Amen.

Rejected – New Testament

"The stone the builders rejected is become the head of the corner."

Mark 12: 10

Years ago a man applied for a job and was rejected, and his application was thrown in the trash. Despondently leaving the interview, he got in his car and decided to stop off at the downtown library where he shared his story with the parking attendant.

"I'm disappointed because I got rejected for a job I wanted."

The attendant said, "God takes the small 'd' in disappointment and makes it a capital 'H' for His appointment."

The man never forgot the words of the parking attendant.

When we are rejected for one thing in the world, God is accepting us for something better.

For one thing, He is strengthening our faith.

Dear Father in Heaven, May this disappointment be turned into Your appointment. Thank You for eliminating undesirable things. Amen.

Other Bible References about Rejection: 1 Samuel 8: 7; Job 42: 6-8; Psalms 19: 14; Isaiah 41: 9; 53: 3; Matthews 27: 30-31; John 6: 37; 12: 48-49; 1 Corinthians 1: 26-28; Hebrews 10: 36; 13: 20-21; 1 Peter 2: 8

Repentance – Old Testament

"I have heard thee by the hearing of the ear, but now my eye seeth thee. wherefore I abhor myself, and repent in dust and ashes."
Job 42: 5-6

Job repented only after meeting God face to face and being interrogated. Meeting God face to face makes us want to repent, for God is an awesome God who is holy and righteous.

But a former preacher of mine said repentance takes place only after the cup of sin has overflowed -- citing the sins of the Amorites (Genesis 15: 16). When iniquities have gone over our heads, we call out for God.

Ezra the priest confirms this when God had him confront the children of Israel about marrying foreign women: he said iniquities had gone over their heads (Ezra 9: 6).

Ezra called a meeting, and upon a proclamation of righteousness, the heads of families agreed to make an end of their foreign marriages and return to the law of God. They repented of evil (Ezra 10).

If sin is overflowing in your life, consider calling on God and acknowledging sin. Humbly accept discipline and agree to obey God and His commandments.

Repentance brings the peace and joy of a new life that pleases God.

Dear Lord, I acknowledge my sin and want to change.
Humble me, O God – to know Your will for my life. Amen.

Repentance – New Testament

When Jesus heard it, he saith unto them, "They that are whole have no need of the physician; but they that are sick. I came not to call the righteous, but sinners to repentance."

Mark 2: 11

Jesus is still calling sinners to repentance because he loves everyone and wants them spared the punishment of sin. An American Indian preacher I knew best illustrated how repentance works. He walked across the church stage only to stop at the far end. He said, "Before you go the other way, you must stop. Repentance works the same way, you stop doing wrong and start doing right." Then he proceeded to walk back to the center of the stage.

Consider stopping in front of God to acknowledge sin and proceed on to righteousness and truth.

Jesus showed us how we should act for repentance when he called a little child out of the crowd and said, "Except ye be converted and become as little children, ye shall not enter into the kingdom of heaven," (Matthew 18: 3).

Dear Father in Heaven, I know I'm doing wrong, and I humble myself before You. Forgive my sin. Allow me to live righteously in Christ Jesus. Amen.

Other Bible References about Repentance: Job 42: 6; Psalms 106: 45; Luke 13: 5, 7; John 8: 9; Acts 1: 5; Hebrews 6: 1-6; Revelation 2: 5

Righteousness – Old Testament

. . . What mean the testimonies, and the statutes, and the judgments, which the Lord our God that commanded you? Then thou shalt say unto thy son, We were Pharaoh's bondmen in Egypt; and the Lord brought us out of Egypt with a mighty hand.

Deuteronomy 6: 20-21

God's laws have the power to free us from oppression as the Israelites but we must be subject to their discipline; otherwise, we may become cursed (Deuteronomy 28: 15-68).

The Bible says, The law of the Lord is perfect, converting the soul; the testimony of the Lord is sure, making wise the simple. The statutes of the Lord are right, rejoicing the heart; the commandment of the Lord is pure, enlightening the eyes ((Psalms 19: 7-8).

Consider also reading Psalm 1, which speaks of two men and two ways: one man seeks the righteousness of God and becomes stable while the other is blown away like chaff in the wind.

Dear Lord, I thank You for your laws, for they guide me in the way I should go. Amen.

Righteousness – New Testament

There is therefore now no condemnation to them which are in Christ Jesus, who walk not after the flesh, but after the spirit. For the law of the Spirit of life in Christ Jesus hath made me free from the law of sin and death.

Romans 8: 1-2

Righteousness in Christ continues to obey the law, for Christ said he did not come to destroy the law but fulfill it (Matthew 5: 17). No jot or tittle would fail – meaning none of the letters or words would be changed in the law.

Christ gives an example of acknowledging the law when he healed the man's paralyzed hand on the Sabbath day, but he incorporated mercy in his actions (Luke 6: 6-10).

Christ said in response to his accusers, "Is it lawful on the Sabbath days to do good, or to do evil; to save life, or destroy it?"

We are to perform righteousness (1 John 3: 10). In fact, we are warned that our righteousness should exceed the righteousness of the scribes and Pharisees (Matthew 5: 20).

But Christ knew the religious law of sacrificial offerings could not completely redeem a person from sin, so he fulfilled God's mission for a new testament of providing his body as a sacrifice.

Dear Father, I thank You for the law which helps guide me and protect me, but I also thank You for Jesus, who died for my sin and frees me to serve You. Amen.

Other Bible References about Righteousness: Job 35: 2; Psalms 37: 16; 92: 13; Proverbs 13: 21; Isaiah 64: 6; Romans 3: 21-31; 5: 18-21; 2 Corinthians 5: 2; 1 Peter 2: 13-14; Revelation 19: 11; Ten Commandments from God: Exodus 20: 3-17; Psalm of righteousness: Psalms 119

Safety – Old Testament

And when the morning arose, the angels hastened Lot, saying, Arise, take thy wife, and thy two daughters, the Lord being merciful unto him: and they brought him forth, and set him without the city.

Genesis 19: 16

Two angels came into Lot's life to save him and his family from a disaster but Lot took his time leaving and the angels had to grab his hand.

When God shows us the way for safety, we should obediently follow. The Bible says, But whoso hearkeneth unto me shall dwell safely, and shall be quiet from fear of evil (Proverbs 1: 33).

Lot then complained about going to a mountain the angels said was safe. Maybe it was too far away, or maybe his family were tired, but God again had mercy and allowed Lot and family to stop at the town of Zoar.

Lot and his family were saved from the wicked town's burning fire except for Lot's wife, who disobeyed the angel's command by looking back at the burning city.

Dear Lord, You are truly my refuge; You are the one I turn to for safety. Have mercy on me, my friends, and family. Amen.

Safety – New Testament

For whosoever shall call upon the name of the Lord shall be saved.

Romans 10: 13

One night I called on the Lord for safety because a terrible fight broke out among the troops in Korea where I was stationed. Soldiers were beating each other with sticks.

But I had no intention of fighting for a vain cause when I was leaving the country in a few weeks, so I called on the Lord for safety and found myself in the back of a pickup truck.

But sometimes we must be still for safety. A year earlier, I had been sitting in a recreation room with friends when an armed man came in and requested everyone to empty their pockets. I again prayed for God's safety.

As it turned out, the man said he was joking. but it was a joke that could have turned deadly because war veterans in the room were ready to retaliate. Trust the Lord to keep you safe. He is our refuge and fortress, and a present help in time of trouble.

Dear Lord, I trust You to keep me safe. And I trust in Christ, who died for my sins for eternal security. Amen.

Other Bible References about Safety: Psalms 4, 5, & 6; 137: 3-5; 118: 8-9; 121: 7-8; Proverbs 3: 24; 18: 10; Micah 7: 5; Matthew 10: 28; John 14: 1-3; 1 Peter 3: 12-14; Wisdom protects from fear of evil: Proverbs 1: 20-33; Blessedness of trusting God: Psalms 146

Salvation – Old Testament

"Truly my soul waiteth upon God; from Him only cometh my salvation."

Psalms 62: 1

Another meaning for the word "waiteth" in the Hebrew transliteration is "silence." ("Only to God in silence is my soul; from Him only comes my salvation.")

If you have salvation, you have nothing to fear. You are saved from illness, disease, war, evil, and judgment -- and you are saved at death.

But if you don't have salvation, now is a good time to silently receive it. Confessing sin, asking forgiveness, and listening to God goes a long way towards receiving salvation.

Dear Lord, "Salvation belongeth unto the Lord: thy blessing is upon thy people. Hear me when I call, O God of my righteousness: thou hast enlarged me when I was in distress; have mercy upon me, and hear my prayer" (Psalms 3: 8-4: 1). Amen.

111

Salvation – New Testament

That if thou shalt confess with the mouth the Lord Jesus, and shalt believe in thine heart that God hath raised him from the dead, thou shalt be saved.

Romans 10: 9

Salvation is available to anyone who calls on the name of the Lord, confesses sin, and accepts Jesus as Savior (Roman 10: 11-21). Jesus is able to give us salvation because he is a perfect sacrifice who went to the cross of death.

Christ says, "Behold, I stand at the door, and knock: if any man hear my voice, and open the door, I will come in to him, and will sup with him, and he with me," (Revelation 3: 20).

The sinful rich man Zaccheus opened the door of his home for Jesus, and Jesus said, "This day is salvation come to this house," (Luke 19: 9).

May we open the door of our lives for Christ to give us salvation.

Dear Lord, I praise you for providing Jesus Christ to take away my sin and give me salvation. Amen.

Other Bible References: Psalms 32, 51; 91; Luke 2: 30, Romans 1: 16; Hebrews 9: 28; 1 John 1: 9

"For thou didst it secretly, but I will do this thing before all Israel, and before the sun."

2 Samuel 12: 12

Not only was God going to expose David's sin before his own people but all over the land. David had secretly lay with another man's wife and then placed him on the front line of a battlefield to be killed.

God knows all our secrets, whether they are good or evil.

If our secrets are good, He may conceal the matter for His glory. Joseph withheld identity from his brothers so they could be fed with grain in time of famine (Genesis 42: 7-9). Abraham withheld identity from King Abimelech to save his life.

But if our secrets are evil, He may expose the matter because He loves us enough to correct us and put us on the right path to enjoy life.

God's secrets are for a good purpose, when we know God.

Dear Lord, There is nothing hidden before You. I confess my secret sins and agree to live an open righteous life. Amen.

Secrets – New Testament

"For nothing is secret that shall not be made manifest, neither anything hid, that shall not be known and come abroad."

Luke 8: 17

The Bible also says, All things are indeed open and naked unto Him with whom we have to do (Hebrews 4: 13). So if we think we have secret sins, which God already knows about, we should confess them to God so we don't have an unnecessary burden to carry around.

But some secrets are to be revealed in God's time, such as when Christ's mother, Mary, kept the sayings of the shepherds in her heart about her baby Jesus being Savior (Luke 2: 6-19). (King Herod was seeking to kill infant children; Matthew 2: 16.)

But the gift that God now gives us in Jesus should be no secret. We should openly proclaim to the world that God has sent a Savior to redeem sin.

Dear Lord, I praise You for taking away my secret sins by Jesus. Now I can live openly with You and share the knowledge of the gospel. Amen.

Other Bible References about Secrets: Deuteronomy 29: 29; Proverbs 25: 2; Psalms 90: 8; Ecclesiastes 12: 13; Isaiah 48: 16; Matthew 5: 14-16; Ephesians 5: 11-13

Sex Relations (unmarried)– Old Testament

And it came to pass after these things, that his master's wife cast her eyes upon Joseph; and she said, "Lie with me."
Genesis 39: 6

Joseph refused to lay down with his master's wife saying it would be a sin against God.

When there is a temptation to have illicit sexual relations, invoke God's name for separation. God is a holy God who wants all our attention on Him rather than a temptation to sin.

The Bible advises a man to stay away from a strange woman (Proverbs 7: 5); lust not after her beauty in thine hearty; neither let her take thee with her eyelids (Proverbs 6: 25).

God's laws concerning improper sexual relations with people or animals are in the Book of Leviticus: Chapters 18-20, and regulations for issues that proceed from man or woman are in Chapter 15.

If a man does have relations with a woman who is not married, he shall surely endow her to be his wife (Exodus 22: 16).

Dear Lord, Thank You for Your Word here that guides me. May I look to please You rather than the lust of the flesh. Amen.

Sex Relations (unmarried) – New Testament

This I say then, "Walk in the Spirit, and ye shall not fulfill the lust of the flesh."

Galatians 5: 16

People who lust after the desires of the flesh can not please God (Romans 8: 8). The Apostle Paul further says there is no good thing in the flesh (Romans 7: 18).

But youthful temptations do take place. Fortunately, God has provided power over those temptations by Jesus who has crucified their sinful lusts (read Romans 8: 3; Galatians 5: 17-24).

To avoid fornication, the Bible also says it is not good for a man to touch a woman (1 Corinthians 7: 1); yet we are advised to let every man have his own wife; and let every woman have her own husband (1 Corinthians 7: 2); it is better to marry than to burn (1 Corinthians 7: 9).

Dear Lord, I praise You for Christ who has power over the lust of the flesh. I will serve You in the spirit of life that gives You glory. Amen.

Other Bible References about Sex and the Body: Exodus 22: 16; Isaiah 52: 11; Matthew 19: 10-12; Romans 7: 4; 1 Corinthians 5: 3; 6: 13-19; 7: 1; Hebrews 13: 4; James 2: 14-15; 2 Peter 2: 9

Sexual Relations (married) – Old Testament

And God blessed them, and God said unto them, "Be fruitful, and multiply . . . ."

Genesis 1: 28

God commanded Adam and Eve to reproduce but it was only after they were disciplined in the Garden of Eden were they able to have children. Adam then knew how to be sensitive to Eve's weakness and emotions, and Eve knew to how to accept Adam's strength and leadership.

The Book of Solomon gives a fine example of love between a man and a woman.

The Shulamite bride speaks of her beloved, "My beloved is mine, and I am his: he feedeth among the lilies. Until the day break, and the shadows flee away, turn, my beloved, and be thou like a roe or a young hart upon the mountain of Bether" (Song of Solomon 2: 16-17).

And the bridegroom adores his bride: "How fair is thy love, my sister, my spouse! How much better is thy love than wine! And the smell of thine ointments than all spices!" (Song of Solomon 4: 10).

Dear Lord, I praise You for my mate. May we nurture each other to enjoy the blessings that come from a commitment to You. Amen.

117

Sex Relations (married) – New Testament

Let the husband render unto the wife due benevolence: and likewise also the wife unto the husband. The wife hath not power of her own body, but the husband: and likewise also the husband hath not power of his own body, but the wife.

1 Corinthians 7: 3-4

A married couple is to serve each other and not selfish pleasure. The Bible says, Defraud ye not one the other, except it be with consent for a time, that ye may give yourselves to fasting and prayer; and come together again, that Satan tempt you not for your incontinency (verse 5).

The Bible further says, Men are to give honor unto the wife as unto the weaker vessel (1 Peter 3: 7). Wives submit yourselves unto your own husbands as unto the Lord (Ephesians 5: 22). Husbands, love your wives, even as Christ also loved the church, and gave himself for it (Ephesians 5: 25).

Look to the Lord for understanding and sensitivity towards your mate. You will be blessed by God.

Marriage is honorable in all, and the bed undefiled (Hebrews 13: 4).

Dear Father in Heaven, Thank You so much for my spouse. May I be sensitive to my mate's needs and You in the spirit. Amen.

Sickness – Old Testament

And the Lord will take away from thee all sickness . . . .
Deuteronomy 7: 15

The Lord takes away all sickness by obedience to His commandments but many of us think going to a doctor, taking drugs, practicing self therapy, or learning psychology will make us well. But only a pure God heals.

In Isaiah's time, prideful King Hezekiah was sick unto death, but Hezekiah humbled himself to God and prayed (Isaiah 38). Hezekiah's sins were cast away (Isaiah 38: 17), and he was made whole. Hezekiah also used a natural remedy of boiled figs (2 Kings 20: 7).

The true God says, "I wound, and I heal" (Deuteronomy 32: 39).

Looking to God, confessing sin, and obeying His commandments goes a long way towards becoming healthy.

Dear Lord, I thank You for showing me how to become well by separating myself to You in complete obedience. I trust only You to make me well. Amen.

Sickness – New Testament

For we have not a high priest which cannot be touched with the feeling of our infirmities; but was in all points tempted like as we are. yet without sin. Let us therefore come boldly unto the throne of grace, that we may obtain mercy, and find grace in time of need.
Hebrews 4: 14-16

Christ can heal us because he is holy and sits on the right hand of God and intercedes for us. But it often takes sickness or injury for us to reach out to him.

A woman, who had an issue of blood for twelve years that no doctor could heal, reached out and touched Jesus and was made whole (Mark 5: 25-34).

Touching Jesus in the heavens makes us whole.

When infection comes, look to Christ for purity. When wounded, look to Christ to bind up. And when apathy comes, look to Christ for strength and resurrection.

Belief and faith in the risen Christ heals.

Dear Lord, I humble myself before You and praise You for Jesus Christ who takes away my sin. Grant me the strength I need to glorify and praise You. Amen.

Other Bible References about Healing: Exodus. 23: 25; Psalms 103: 1-4; Proverbs 17: 22; 24: 10; Isaiah 35: 3; 52: 4; 57: 14; 58: 8-9; Jeremiah. 17: 14; Matthew 4: 23-24; 11: 28-30; Luke 9: 1: James 5: 16

Sin – Old Testament

For Achan . . . of the tribe of Judah . . . took of the accursed thing: and the anger of the Lord was kindled against the children of Israel.

Joshua 7: 1

God had commanded the victorious army of Israel to abandon the accursed goods of Jericho except the silver and gold which was to be put in the Lord's treasury. But Achan took some goods -- and the army was defeated in its next battle. Sin was in the camp.

Sin will defeat us and the community if we don't confess it.

A psalmist's prayer helps us to avoid future sin: Keep back thy servant also from presumptuous sins; let them not have dominion over me . . . (Psalm 19: 13).

We might also take Solomon's advice in the Book of Proverbs: He that covereth his sins shall not prosper but whoso confesseth and forsaketh them, shall have mercy (Proverbs 28: 13).

Now is a good time to confess sin and ask for God's mercy.

Dear Lord, I am sorry that I have sinned. Please take away my sins and grant me mercy. I am willing to recompense that which I sinned against. Amen.

Sin – New Testament

What shall we say then? Is the law sin? Nay, I had not known sin but by the law; for I had not known lust, except the law had said, Thou shalt not covet.

Romans 7: 7

The law convicts us of sin. We have compared our actions with the law and we are guilty.

Fortunately, God has provided Jesus as a sacrifice for our sin.

If we say we have no sin, we make a God a liar (1 John 1: 10). All men have sinned, and come short of the glory of God (Romans 3: 23).

Sin causes us and other people to suffer, but it helps to know God loves whom He corrects (Hebrews 12: 8-11), and we should be open to His discipline so we can lead a good life.

Dear Lord, I acknowledge my sin before You. Have mercy on me by Christ Jesus, who died for my sin. Forgive me and I shall be forgiven and I will testify of your salvation and mercy forever. Amen.

Other Bible References about Sin: Numbers 32: 23; Psalms 25: 6, 7; 51: 1-4; Isaiah 53: 6; Ezekiel 36: 25-26; Acts 10: 43; Romans 6: 11; 10:8: 2 Corinthians 5: 17-18; I John 2: 1-2; 3: 5; Hebrews 10: 14; 1 Peter 2: 24

Sports – Old Testament

I have stuck unto thy testimonies; O Lord, put me not to shame. I will run the way of thy commandments, when thou shalt enlarge my heart.

Psalms 119: 31-32

Other than men warring, the people rising up to play around a golden calf, and the strong man Samson being paraded by the lords of the Philistines, sporting of the physical body is non-existent in the Bible.

Our bodies are to be used for His service, such as nursing the sick, feeding the poor, and sheltering the homeless.

God has said, Thou shalt have no other god's before me (Exodus 20: 3), and that would include balls, goal posts, nets, and fences.

We are not to bow down nor worship false gods who can not think, see, nor hear (Exodus 20: 5; Daniel 5: 23).

God is our true bread for life.

Dear Father in Heaven, May this body be used for Your humble service. I bow before You and worship in holiness and truth. Amen.

Know ye not that they who run in a race run all, but one receiveth the prize? So run, that ye may obtain. Now every man that striveth for the mastery is temperate in all things. Now they do it to obtain a corruptible crown, but we, an incorruptible.

1 Corinthians 9: 24-25

Receiving a trophy in sports competition for successfully finishing above other competitors is a great feeling, but receiving a crown of glory from God through Jesus Christ for the gift of eternal life is the best prize of all: it never deteriorates.

Our bodies are to be used for God's glory (1 Corinthians 6: 19-20). Constructing housing for the homeless, cooking for the hungry, and transporting the disabled are just a few ways to witness and testify for God, but if we are sporting them for personal recognition, we are not glorifying God.

God may cause us suffer injury or defeat to know that He is God.

The Bible says, For bodily exercise profiteth little: but godliness is profitable unto all things . . . (1 Timothy 4: 8).

Dear Lord, May my body be used for Your purpose and glory. Have mercy upon me to serve You. Amen.

Strength – Old Testament

And Samson lay till midnight, and arose at midnight, and took the doors of the gate of the city, and the two posts, and went away with them, bar and all, and put them upon his shoulders, and carried them up to the top of a hill that is before Hebron.

Judges 16: 3

Samson was a physically strong man carrying the front gate materials up a hill. (He had also torn a lion in pieces, caught 300 foxes, and slayed a thousand Philistines.) But spiritually, Samson was weak. He told his girlfriend Delilah the secret of his strength. She told the lords of the Philistines who hired men to come and shave Samson's hair. (Samson had vowed as a Nazarene to not have his hair shaven (Numbers 6: 1). And Samson was weakened and imprisoned.

It is by God that we can receive strength (Psalms 68: 34-35), but if we have turned away from God, we have lost our strength. David the psalmist said, My strength faileth because of mine iniquity (Psalms 31: 10).;

Confessing our sins and coming into agreement with God strengthens our lives. Upon forgiveness, we are free to serve the living God in sincerity and truth.

Be reminded there was not one feeble person among the Israelites who came into the land of God's promise (Psalms 105: 37). Seek the Lord and His strength: seek His face evermore (Psalms 105: 4). However, if thou faint in the day of adversity, thy strength is small (Proverbs 24: 10).

Dear Lord, Feed me the food which makes me strong, yet feed me Your word which makes me wise unto salvation and life. Amen.

125

Strength – New Testament

I can do all things with Christ who strengtheneth me.

Philippians 4: 13

Christ gives us strength because he takes away our sins and has power over Satan. In different words, he can take away the troubles that cause us to work in vain so we can spend more time gathering strength to work for God in the Spirit.

The Apostle Paul said he would rather be weak, knowing that he was closer to God: "Therefore, I take pleasure in infirmities, in reproaches, in necessities, in persecutions, in distresses for Christ's sake: for when I am weak, then am I strong " (2 Corinthians 12: 9-10).

Yet we do pray for God to give us our daily bread, and eating a good meal gives us physical strength to work for God.(For one believeth that he may eat all things: another, who is weak, eateth herbs; Romans 14: 2).

Be reminded Jesus said man shall not live by bread alone but by every word that proceedeth out of the mouth of God (Matthew 4: 4).

And when Paul was experiencing pain, Christ came into his life and said, "My grace is sufficient for thee; for my strength is made perfect in weakness (1 Corinthians 12: 9).

Dear Father in Heaven. I thank You for the strength in Christ Jesus who is risen and inspires me to become stronger. I also thank You also for removing a burden of sin by my confession and humbleness. Amen.

Other Bible References: Leviticus 26: 40; Psalms 22: 26; 37: 26; 71: 16; 84: 5; Proverbs 18: 10; 24: 10, 15; Luke 2: 40; Ephesians 3: 16; 6: 10; Hebrews 8: 10; Sin saps strength: Psalms 31: 10

Stress – Old Testament

And it came to pass on the morrow, that Moses sat to judge the people: and the people stood by Moses from the morning to evening.

Exodus 18: 13

Moses was experiencing a lot of stress judging all the affairs of the people, so his father-in-law Jethro told him to appoint some more judges.

We may have to take someone else's advice when experiencing stress; otherwise, our pride may break us down.

Consider also reading Psalm 107 which shows the children of Israel suffering from stress. There was overwork, wandering, confusion, and sin, yet the psalmist extolled God's goodness and mercy through it all.

Another psalmist said, The Lord heard his voice and supplications, and he was given rest (Psalms 116: 1-7).

Dear Lord, Have mercy on me and forgive me for being so prideful. You are my first desire, and I lay down my pride to accept Your will for my life. Amen.

"Come unto me, all ye that labor and are heavy laden, and I will give you rest. Take my yoke upon you, and learn of me: for I am meek and lowly in heart: and ye shall find rest unto your souls. For my yoke is easy, and my burden is light."

Matthew 11: 28-30

Jesus had a light burden because he had no sin and his yoke was easy because it was attached to his Father in Heaven.

We should have such an attachment to God's peace and rest.

The scriptures encourage us to cease from our own works -- as God did from his -- from the foundation of the world (read Hebrews 4: 10).

But consider this man Jesus who made himself of no reputation, and took upon him the form of a servant (Philippians 2: 7). He gives us rest from stress and freedom from sin.

Dear Lord, I praise You for Jesus who takes away my sin to give me rest. Have mercy upon me. Amen.

Other Bible References: Romans 9: 16; Galatians 6: 5

Suicide – Old Testament

See, I have set before thee this day, life and good, and death and evil.

Deuteronomy 30: 15.

Moses put a choice of life and death before the people to test their faith, and God often puts the same choice before us.

If we choose life, we testify of God's saving presence and glory, but if we choose death, we can not praise God from the grave (Psalms 6: 5; 88: 10).

Joshua later also gave the people an ultimatum: "And if seem evil to you to serve the Lord, choose you this day whom ye will serve" (Joshua 24: 15).

The people responded, "The Lord our God will we serve, and his voice will we obey" (Joshua 24: 24).

Serving God can be our life when we call upon Him in faith and commitment.

God commands us not to kill (Exodus 20: 13), which includes us as well as other people. To do so would invite the wrath of God.

Dear Lord, "For thou hast delivered my soul from death; mine eyes from tears, and my feet from falling. I will walk before the Lord in the land of the living" (Psalms 116: 8-9). Amen.

129

Suicide – New Testament

"For God so loved the world that he gave his only begotten Son, that whosoever believeth in him should not perish, but have everlasting life."

John 3: 16

Christ has already died for us so we might have life but it often takes a near death experience until we find Christ.

Christ said, "He that findeth his life shall lose it, and that loseth his life for my sake shall find it" (Matthew 10: 39). May we give up our life to the living Christ and serve God in the spirit.

The Apostle Paul thought of dying when he was troubled, yet he did not trust in himself but trusted in God who raises the dead (2 Corinthians 1: 8-9).

Christ Jesus gives us power over death (1 Corinthians 15: 54-57). The last enemy death has been defeated.

He is risen, and can be risen with him by belief.

Dear Lord, I humbly accept the risen Christ by the confession of sin into my heart and life. I am renewed in the spirit of my mind to live for You. For whosoever shall call upon the name of the Lord shall be saved (Romans 10: 13). Amen.

Other Bible References: Genesis 3: 22; Deuteronomy 4: 1; Job 2: 6; Psalms 16: 11; 27: 1; 34: 6; 118: 17-18; Isaiah 42: 7; John 10: 10; 11: 25; 16: 33; Romans 10: 13; Ephesians 4: 8-10; Hebrews 12: 9

Terror – Old Testament

And Mount Sinai was altogether on a smoke, because the Lord descended upon it in fire: and the smoke thereof ascended as the smoke of a furnace, and the whole mount quaked greatly.

Exodus 19: 18

God shakes the earth, floods the valleys, and thunders in the skies but He is in the midst of it and He wants us to keep our distance.

He told the people to stay back -- that only Aaron the priest and Moses could proceed.

When powerful events happen, look for God in the middle of them. God can be a consuming fire and He gets jealous over His people for worshipping other gods (Deuteronomy 4: 24-26).

Moses comforted the people and said God was testing their faith -- to see if they would fear Him.

Dear Lord, I know You are a mighty God and worthy to be feared. Have mercy upon me as I draw close to You and seek Your will. Amen.

Terror – New Testament

"For nation shall rise against nation, and kingdom against kingdom; and there shall be famines, pestilences, and earthquakes in divers places."

Matthew 24: 7

Jesus says terrible events may end the world and mankind and he warns to be prepared, such as five brides waiting to see their bridegroom in the dark: the brides had their oil ready to burn for the lamps to shine (Matthew 25: 1-13).

The advent of terrifying events makes us want to be prepared, for God to save us. So we should get to know God and Jesus.

Jesus comforts us saying he will be in the midst of terror -- in the clouds of heaven with great power and glory (Matthew 24: 31).

Consider humbling yourself under the mighty hand of God to accept Jesus. He has promised to be with us to the end (Matthew 28: 20).

Take comfort in knowing there is nothing that has happened that has not happened before (1 Peter 4: 12). We are not to be scared of are man's terror, who can only kill the body (1 Peter 3: 14); but we are to fear God, who can destroy body and soul in hell (Matthew 10: 28).

Dear Lord, I thank You for Jesus in my life. I know I have safety in heaven regardless of what happens in the world, for Jesus has prepared a place for me. Establish peace I pray, all over the world. Amen.

Other Bible References: Psalms 65, 68, 91: 5-6; Joel 2: 10-11

Thankfulness – Old Testament

Oh, give thanks unto the Lord, for he is good; for his mercy endureth forever.

Psalms 136: 1

God is worthy to be thanked because He gives us peace and his mercy endures forever.

We might return thanks by offering the first profits from our investments, serving the public, or doing good deeds for neighbors. But the greatest thanks we can give is dedicating our life to Him.

King David gave his life to God and said a lengthy prayer that thanked Him (I Chronicles 16: 7-36).

If we do not acknowledge God, nor thank Him, He may not acknowledge us (2 Chronicles 15: 2).

The Bible says, Offer unto God thanksgiving, and pay thy vows unto the Most High, and call upon me in the day of trouble; I will deliver thee, and thou shalt glorify me (Psalms 50: 14-15).

Dear Lord, I thank you for Your presence here and praise Your holy name. You are good and Your mercy endures forever. Amen.

Thankfulness – New Testament

Giving thanks always for all things unto God and the Father in the name of our Lord Jesus Christ.

Ephesians 5: 20

Thank you God for providing a Savior to take away our sins and provides everlasting life, yet Jesus says we should also receive thanks.

"For if ye love them who love you, what thanks have ye? For sinners also love those who love them. And if ye do good to them who do good to you, what thanks have ye? For sinners also do even the same" (Luke 6: 32-33).

Feeding the poor, nursing the impoverished, and sharing God's word with the illiterate are ways to receive thanks

While we perform good deeds for the needy (James 1: 22-25), may we continue to give the sacrifice of praise to God continually, that is the fruit of *our* lips giving thanks (Hebrews 13: 15).

Dear Lord, Thank You for Jesus who died for me so that I can serve You. May I give thanks everyday in my words, tithes, and deeds. Amen.

Other Bible References: 1 Chronicles 16: 8; Psalms 35: 18; Psalms 66; 75: 1; 95: 2; 100: 4-5; 1 Corinthians. 15: 57; Colossians 3: 1; Philippians 4: 6

" . . . For the Lord thy God is with thee whithersoever thou goest."

Joshua 1: 9

God gave those words to Joshua shortly after he assumed command of the children of Israel three days before the people were to cross the Jordan river into a strange land.

Knowing God is with us gives us courage to travel to strange destinations.

However, we are warned that the sight [from] the eyes is better than the wandering of the desire (Ecclesiastes 6: 9). We can enjoy God's presence right here in prayer and fellowship.

But if we have to travel, may we look to God for guidance.

The children of Israel crossed the Jordan river into a prosperous land.

He will lead us in righteousness, and will comfort, feed, and protect us, but we must call on His name for help.

Dear Lord, I thank You for being here and in my destination. Provide me with necessary provisions and keep me safe. Amen.

Travel – New Testament

And it came to pass, afterward, that he went throughout every city and village, preaching and showing the glad tidings of the kingdom of God; and the twelve were with him.

Luke 8: 1

Jesus did a lot of traveling witnessing for God but he encountered lots of delays such as we. He me people with demons and illnesses, and lawyers, soldiers, and priests asked him questions. But Jesus took the time to minister to each of their needs.

When we travel, we should look forward to being compassionate towards other people and expressing God's love.

The Bible says to forbear one another in love (Ephesians 4: 2; Colossians 3: 13). Forbear in those passages means to "hold up."

May we prepare in advance for travel by acquiring necessary provisions but also gather material to witness for God and Christ.

The love for Jesus transcends all people and cultures.

Dear Father, Your word of life is commissioned to be spread all over the world. May everyone know about Jesus. Have mercy on me when I travel. Amen.

Other Bible References about Travel: Psalms 23; Proverbs 27: 8; Matthew 10: 9-10; 28: 19; John 14: 2-3, 23; Hebrews 13: 5

But he knoweth the way that I take: when he hath tried me, I shall come forth as gold. My foot hath held his steps, his way have I kept, and not declined.

Job 23: 10-11

Job stayed around God's throne regardless of the troubles he was having and he was eventually healed of his disease.

We should be so faithful when troubles come, for we do not want to doubt the plan God has for our lives (read Psalms 78 and 95).

Other saints of God were as faithful as Job. Abraham was about to sacrifice his son on an altar but by obedience to God he found an animal sacrifice (Genesis 22: 1-14). Daniel was put in a den of lions but he kept his faith in God for safety (Daniel 6: 16-23).

Life is full of trials that test our faith in God, but at the end of the journey, He will fulfill the promise.

Dear Father in Heaven, I praise You for being here and saving me from sin. You have control over this situation and I praise You for keeping me humble and righteous. Amen.

137

Trials – New Testament

That the trial of your faith, being much more precious than of gold that perisheth, though it be tried with fire, might be found unto praise and honor and glory at the appearing of Jesus Christ.

1 Peter 1: 7

Our faith in God is confronted with temptations to sin but trusting Jesus and reading the Scriptures helps us overcome temptation.

When Jesus was faced with temptation, he rejected it and quoted scripture: Thou shalt not tempt the Lord, thy God (Matthew 4: 7).

The concordances found in most Bibles provide reference Scriptures that apply to the temptation and reveal God's word of victory.

When the Devil presents a temptation to do wrong, reject it and turn to Jesus for the power to overcome it.

The Bible says, My brethren, count it all joy when ye fall into divers temptations, Knowing this, that the trying of your faith worketh patience (James 1: 2-3).

Dear Lord, Thank You for Your Son Jesus, who has victory over evil. May I follow the plan You have for my life that is good and gives You glory. Amen.

Truth – Old Testament

God is not a man that he should lie; neither the son of man that he should repent. Hath he said and shall he not do it? Or hath he spoken and shall he not make it good?

Numbers 23: 19

God can be trusted because He fulfills His obligations. Man can not be trusted because he can not always fulfill promises. Therefore, we look to God for truth.

Deuteronomy 32: 4 says He is the rock, his work is perfect; for all his ways are judgment; a God of truth and without iniquity, just and right is he.

We need this God because we are prone to sin. God has provided rules and regulations in the first five books of the Bible to guide us. It's up to us to trust and obey Him.

The leaders of the children of Israel who entered God's land of promise gave testimony of God's faithfulness.

And the Psalmists praised the God of truth: Thy righteousness is an everlasting righteousness, and thy law is the truth (Psalms 119: 142). Lead me in thy truth, teach me, for thou art the God of my salvation, on thee do I wait all the day (Psalms 25: 5).

All the paths of the Lord are mercy and truth unto such as keep his covenant and his testimonies (Psalm 25: 10).

Dear Lord, I thank You for providing your record of truth in the Old Testament. Your word is truly a lamp unto my feet and a light unto my path. Amen.

Truth – New Testament

Jesus saith unto him, I am the way, the truth, and the life . . . .
John 14: 6

Truth records in the New Testament that the Gentiles needed a Savior so God sent His son Jesus in the form and lineage of the first man Adam to be a sacrifice for the sins of the people.

Jesus was born of a virgin woman and did not sin. Yet he died for the people's sins and rose into heaven on the third day. He now intercedes for the people. Truth further records men who refuse to accept Christ as the living Savior are the anti-Christ.

This is the beginning of finding full truth: that man is prone to make errors and needs a divine Savior like Jesus for sanctification. (If we say we have not sinned, we make God a liar; 1 John 1: 10.)

According to Jesus, those who worship God are to worship in spirit and truth (John 4: 24). but Jesus also says, "No man cometh to the Father but by me." (John 14: 26). Upon confession of Jesus, God sends us the Spirit of truth (John 14: 17; 15-26-27; 16: 13).

Dear Lord, I praise You for the truth that comes by Jesus. Forgive my sins and sanctify me by this truth. Amen.

Other Bible References: Deuteronomy 11: 16; Psalms 25: 5; 31: 5; 119: 151, 160; John 3: 11; 4: 24; 8: 14-18, 31-32; 16: 13 ; 2 Timothy 2: 11; Hebrews. 6: 18; 1 John 4: 6; True light from God sent from John the Baptist: John 1: 18

War – Old Testament

The Lord is a man of war; the Lord is His name.

Exodus 15: 3

God wars for righteousness and glory but many of us war for selfish interests such as land, money, material, or people.

We are warned in God's law not to covet anything from a neighbor (Exodus 20:17), nor oppress strangers (Exodus 22: 21). Violations of these precepts often lead to war.

We are to rebuke a person in righteousness (Leviticus 19: 17).

But often, the war is within ourselves: one part of us wants to do one thing while the other the opposite.

May we humble ourselves from personal war and seek the peace that comes from God by confession of sin and obedience to the law.

God creates war, but He also makes war to cease (Psalms 46: 9).

Dear Lord, You are in charge of war, and Your righteousness and glory will prevail. May the people be spared of violence to worship You and bow down before Your power. Amen.

War – New Testament

Then said Jesus unto him, "Put up again thy sword into its place; for all they that take up the sword perish by the sword."

Matthew 26: 52

Christ gives us wisdom saying that if we use weapons, they will be used against us, but Christ does make war.

According to the author of the Book of Revelation, he wars from heaven in righteousness (Revelation 19: 11).

The soldier Saul gives us a good example of becoming a victim of Christ when he was riding down the road one day and Christ confronted him (Acts 9: 1-20).

Humiliated and disabled, Saul followed and preached Jesus.

The war continues to spread the good news about Jesus.

For he is our peace, who hath made both one, and hath broken down the middle wall of partition between us (Ephesians 2: 14).

Dear Lord, I thank You for Jesus who has overcome the lust of the flesh and the war within. He allows me to love all of humanity. May I refrain from arguing and fighting and seek this peace that passes all understanding. Amen.

Other Bible References: Deuteronomy 20; Proverbs 20: 18; James 4: 1; 1 Peter 2: 11; 3: 10-11

Wisdom – Old Testament

The fear of the Lord is the beginning of wisdom, but fools despise knowledge and instruction.

Proverbs 1: 7

Fearing God is the beginning of wisdom because He has power over our souls. Understanding He is the teacher puts us in the right place to learn, for with the lowly is wisdom (Proverbs 11: 2).

The wisdom books of the Bible are considered to be Job, Psalms, Proverbs, Ecclesiastes, and the Song of Solomon. The characteristics of wisdom are listed in Proverbs 1-9.

God's wisdom saved Abraham from Melchizedek's army, got Joseph out of jail, and taught Jacob to multiply cattle, Noah was instructed how to build an ark, and Nehemiah rebuilt temple walls.

We are encouraged to seek wisdom while it may be found; otherwise, we are warned, God will not answer us when anguish and distress come (Proverbs 1; 24-32).

Dear Lord, You have the wisdom, and I humble myself from my own wisdom to listen to You for discernment, prosperity, and safety. Have mercy on me I pray. Amen.

Wisdom – New Testament

For the wisdom of this world is foolishness with God. For it is written, He taketh the wise in their own craftiness.

1 Corinthians 3: 19

Wisdom of this world is earthly, sensual, and devilish (James 3: 15). But the wisdom that comes from above is first pure, then peaceable . . . (James 3: 17).

This is the wisdom we need, which enables us to profit spiritually and have peace.

Man would have you believe wisdom comes from worldly textbooks and personal thought, but the Lord knoweth the thoughts of the wise, that they are vain (1 Corinthians 3: 20).

The mystery of receiving great wisdom is explained in the 2nd Chapter of 1 Corinthians:

Now we have received not the spirit of the world, but the spirit which is of God . . . (1 Corinthians 2: 12). The Spirit searcheth all things, yea, the deep things of God (1 Corinthians 2: 10).

If any of you lack wisdom, let him ask of God, that giveth to all *men* liberally, and upbraideth not; and it shall be given him (James 1: 5).

But the greatest wisdom we can have is that which grants personal salvation (2 Timothy 3: 15).

Dear Lord, I thank You for the wisdom in the Holy Scriptures that show me how to live and receive Your blessings. The greatest wisdom I can have is receiving Your Son Jesus who saves my soul. Amen.

Other Bible References: Proverbs 2: 6; 8: 17; 23: 4; Ecclesiastes 1: 18; 1 Corinthians 1: 19; Colossians 2: 3; James 1: 5; 1 Timothy 2: 15

Work – Old Testament

And the Lord took the man, and put him into the garden of Eden, to dress it, and to till it.

Genesis 2: 15

Man was put on earth to freely work and multiply but he disobeyed God's command by eating from the tree of knowledge of good and evil and was condemned to work by the sweat of his face (Genesis 3: 17-19).

Nevertheless, the Bible says it is a gift from God to work: There is nothing better for a man . . . that he should make his soul enjoy good in his labor (Ecclesiastes. 2:24).

But the first job we have is to know the true God by studying the law, ordinances, and commandments; then we know who we are working for and what to do. (Otherwise, we may be enslaved to another god; read Deuteronomy 4: 23-28.)

If we don't want to work, the Bible says we may hunger (Proverbs 19: 15). Nevertheless, more wisdom from the Book of Proverbs states: Labor not to be rich; cease from thine own wisdom (Proverbs 23: 4); but in all labor, there is profit (Proverbs 14: 23).

Dear Lord, I praise You for letting me work for Your good purpose. Perfect the work that You have begun in me to produce good things, and may all this work glorify You. Amen.

145

"Verily, verily, I say unto you, He that believeth on me, the works that I do shall he do also. . . ."

John 14: 12

The disciples saw the works that Jesus performed and asked, "What shall we do, that we might work the works of God?"

Jesus answered and said unto them, "This is the work of God, that ye might believe on him whom he hath sent" (John 6: 29).

Believing in Jesus gives us access to God's good works. We have the power of healing, teaching, nursing, ministering, constructing, and miracles. But if we don't know God through Jesus, our works are in vain. They are selfish works which will reap little satisfaction.

The Bible says we should be working our way towards salvation (.Philippians 2: 9-16),

Dear Lord, I praise You for showing me the work You want me to do. Perfect that which concerns me and may Your work prosper. Amen.

Other Bible References about Work: Genesis 3: 19; 2 Chronicles 15: 7; Psalms 111: 2; 138: 8; Proverbs 10: 4-5; 16: 3; 21: 25; Ecclesiastes 2: 4-7; 9: 10; Luke 2: 49; John 15: 4-5; Galatians 2: 16; 6: 4; Ephesians 2: 8-10; 4: 1; Philippians 1: 6; 4: 13; 2 Thessalonians 3: 10-12; James 2: 14-26.

Worry – Old Testament

God is our refuge and strength, a very present help in trouble. Therefore will not we fear; though the earth be removed, and the mountains carried into the midst of the sea.

Psalms 46: 1-2

Psalm 46 comforts us because it shows God is in control regardless of what happens to the earth, but there is more wisdom to relieve our worries.

We are not to worry about the next day (Proverbs 27: 1). We are not to worry about the weather (Ecclesiastes 11: 4). We do not to worry about other countries, for He ruleth by his power forever; his eyes behold the nations. (Psalms 66: 7). Neither are we to worry about man (Psalms 56: 4).

But we have plenty to worry about if we do not know God. The sinner David said of his sin, "I am troubled; I am bowed down greatly; I go mourning all the day long" (Psalm 38: 6).

We do not want to be troubled like David so let's make sure sin is confessed for mercy and life (Proverbs 28: 15).

Knowing God is in control relieves our worries, but it takes our faith to know God. The Psalmist finishes Psalm 46 saying, Be still, and know that I am God . . . (verse 10).

Dear Lord, With You as comforter, I can face this anxiety and feel calm. May I patiently seek this cause for worry and have it removed, for I am saved by faith and trust in You. Amen.

Worry – New Testament

*Therefore, take no thought saying, What shall we eat? or,
What shall we drink? or, With what shall we be clothed?*

Matthew 6: 31

Much of our worry is about food, drink, or clothing, but Jesus encourages us to trust in God for all these things. We are first to seek the kingdom of God and His righteousness, and those things will be added unto us.

But other things cause us to worry: nearby wars, technological hazards, environmental pollution, and illness are causes for concern.

Knowing God has control over these issues comforts us. The world is subject to God (Revelation 14: 7). Man is subject to Christ (1 Peter 3: 22). If we know both God and Christ, we will not worry.

We might take some of the Apostle Paul's advice and be {anxious} for nothing, but in everything, by prayer and supplication with thanksgiving, let your requests be made known unto God (Philippians 4: 6).

And the peace of God, which passeth all understanding, shall keep your hearts and mind through Christ Jesus (verse 7).

Dear Lord, Thank you for increasing my faith. I know that You are in control of this situation and I look to You for the right thing to do. Amen.

Other Bible References: 1 Peter 5: 10

Worship – Old Testament

"Thou shalt have no other gods before me. Thou shalt not make unto thee any graven image, or any likeness of anything that is in heaven above, or that is in the earth beneath, or that is in the water under the earth; Thou shalt not bow down thyself to them, nor serve them . . . ."

Exodus 20: 3-5

God tells by His first commandment that He has priority over all other gods, and rightly so: He forgives and redeems sins. He creates and destroys life. He grants prosperity or poverty, and He gives good or bad health.

So He wants worship, and we are commanded to love Him with all [our] heart, and with all [our] soul, and with all [our] might (Deuteronomy 6: 5).

Psalms 95 exhorts us to worship: O come, let us worship and bow down: let us kneel before the Lord our maker. For He is our God; and we are the sheep of His pasture . . . (verse 5-6).

When the patriarch Jacob and company went to worship God at Bethel, they were to put away their strange gods and get clean (Genesis 35).

That's what we need to do: put away strange gods and get clean. God is holy, and we are to be holy with Him. And wherever God wants us to worship, we are to worship Him in spirit and truth.

Dear Lord, My praise shall be of Thee in the great congregation: I will pay my vows before them that fear him. The meek shall eat and be satisfied: they shall praise the Lord that seek him; your heart shall live for ever; (Psalms 22: 25-26). Amen.

Worship – New Testament

Blessing, and honor, and glory, and power be unto him that sitteth upon the throne, and unto the Lamb forever and ever.

Revelation 5: 13

Jesus is worthy to be worshipped because he is the Son of God who arose from the dead and now sits in the heavens on the right hand of God to intercede for us.

The Bible says, but this man, because he continueth forever . . . is also able to save them to the uttermost that come unto God by him, seeing he ever liveth to make intercession for them (Hebrews 7: 24-25).

Christ is at the door to the temple of God in heaven, and if we hear his voice and open the door, he will come into us and dine with us (Revelation 3: 20).

Dear Lord, I praise You for Jesus in the congregation of saints. You have provided a great sacrifice for our sins. Amen.

Other Bible References about Worshipping: Psalms 22: 25-26; 95: 6; 138: 2; Ecclesiastes. 5: 1-2;Daniel 5: 23; Matthew 25: 33-34; John 3: 3; 4: 23-24; Acts 7: 48-49; 1 Corinthians 3: 16; Colossians 2: 8-9